COLLECTED POEMS

COLLECTED POEMS
1974–2004
RITA DOVE

W. W. NORTON & COMPANY

INDEPENDENT PUBLISHERS SINCE 1923

NEW YORK LONDON

Manufacturing by RR Donnelley, Harrisonburg, VA
Book design by JAM Design
Production manager: Anna Oler

ISBN 978-0-393-28594-9

W. W. Norton & Company, Inc.
500 Fifth Avenue, New York, N.Y. 10110
www.wwnorton.com

W. W. Norton & Company Ltd.
Castle House, 75/76 Wells Street, London W1T 3QT

1 2 3 4 5 6 7 8 9 0

Fred, always

CONTENTS

In the Old Neighborhood   *3*

THE YELLOW HOUSE ON THE CORNER (1980)   *9*

I

This Life   *13*
The Bird Frau   *13*
Robert Schumann, Or: Musical Genius Begins with Affliction   *14*
Happenstance   *15*
Small Town   *15*
The Snow King   *16*
Sightseeing   *16*
Upon Meeting Don L. Lee, In a Dream   *18*
"Teach Us to Number Our Days"   *18*
Nigger Song: An Odyssey   *19*

II

Five Elephants   *23*
Geometry   *23*
Champagne   *24*
Night Watch   *24*
The Secret Garden   *25*
A Suite for Augustus
       1963   *25*
       D.C.   *26*
       Planning the Perfect Evening   *26*
       Augustus Observes the Sunset   *27*
       Wake   *28*
       Back   *28*

III

Belinda's Petition   *31*
The House Slave   *31*
David Walker (1785–1830)   *32*
The Abduction   *33*
The Transport of Slaves from Maryland to Mississippi   *34*
Pamela   *35*

Someone's Blood   *36*
Cholera   *36*
The Slave's Critique of Practical Reason   *37*
Kentucky, 1833   *38*

IV
Adolescence—I   *43*
Adolescence—II   *43*
Adolescence—III   *44*
The Boast   *44*
The Kadava Kumbis Devise a Way to Marry for Love   *45*
Spy   *46*
First Kiss   *46*
Then Came Flowers   *47*
Pearls   *47*
Nexus   *47*

V
Notes from a Tunisian Journal   *51*
The Sahara Bus Trip   *51*
For Kazuko   *53*
Beauty and the Beast   *53*
His Shirt   *54*
Great Uncle Beefheart   *55*
The Son   *56*
Corduroy Road   *57*
Ö   *58*

MUSEUM (1983)   *59*

I. THE HILL HAS SOMETHING TO SAY   *61*
The Fish in the Stone   *63*
The Ants of Argos   *64*
Pithos   *64*
Nestor's Bathtub   *65*
The Hill Has Something to Say   *66*
The Copper Beech   *67*
Tou Wan Speaks to Her Husband, Liu Sheng   *68*
Catherine of Alexandria   *69*
Catherine of Siena   *70*

Receiving the Stigmata   *70*
Boccaccio: The Plague Years   *71*
Fiammetta Breaks Her Peace   *72*

II. IN THE BULRUSH   *75*
November for Beginners   *77*
Reading Hölderlin on the Patio with the Aid of a Dictionary   *77*
Shakespeare Say   *78*
Three Days of Forest, a River, Free   *80*
Banneker   *81*
In the Bulrush   *82*
Delft   *83*
Ike   *84*
Agosta the Winged Man and Rasha the Black Dove   *84*
At the German Writers Conference in Munich   *86*

III. MY FATHER'S TELESCOPE   *89*
Grape Sherbet   *91*
Roses   *92*
Sunday Night at Grandfather's   *93*
Centipede   *94*
My Father's Telescope   *94*
Song. Summer   *95*
Anti-Father   *96*
To Bed   *97*
A Father out Walking on the Lawn   *97*

IV. PRIMER FOR THE NUCLEAR AGE   *99*
The Sailor in Africa   *101*
Early Morning on the Tel Aviv–Haifa Freeway   *105*
Why I Turned Vegetarian   *105*
Eastern European Eclogues   *106*
Flirtation   *107*
Exeunt the Viols   *108*
The Left-Handed Cellist   *109*
Lines Muttered in Sleep   *109*
Primer for the Nuclear Age   *109*
Parsley   *110*

THOMAS AND BEULAH (1986) *113*

I. MANDOLIN *115*
The Event *117*
Variation on Pain *118*
Jiving *118*
Straw Hat *119*
Courtship *120*
Refrain *121*
Variation on Guilt *122*
Nothing Down *123*
The Zeppelin Factory *125*
Under the Viaduct, 1932 *126*
Lightnin' Blues *127*
Compendium *128*
Definition in the Face of Unnamed Fury *128*
Aircraft *129*
Aurora Borealis *130*
Variation on Gaining a Son *131*
One Volume Missing *131*
The Charm *132*
Gospel *133*
Roast Possum *134*
The Stroke *135*
The Satisfaction Coal Company *136*
Thomas at the Wheel *138*

II. CANARY IN BLOOM *139*
Taking in Wash *141*
Magic *141*
Courtship, Diligence *142*
Promises *143*
Dusting *144*
A Hill of Beans *145*
Weathering Out *146*
Motherhood *147*
Anniversary *148*
The House on Bishop Street *148*
Daystar *149*
Obedience *150*

The Great Palaces of Versailles   *150*

Pomade   *152*

Headdress   *153*

Sunday Greens   *154*

Recovery   *155*

Nightmare   *155*

Wingfoot Lake   *156*

Company   *157*

The Oriental Ballerina   *158*

Chronology   *160*

GRACE NOTES (1989)   *163*

Summit Beach, 1921   *165*

I

Silos   *169*

Fifth Grade Autobiography   *169*

The Buckeye   *170*

Quaker Oats   *171*

Flash Cards   *172*

Crab-Boil   *172*

Hully Gully   *173*

Fantasy and Science Fiction   *174*

Sisters   *175*

Uncle Millet   *175*

Poem in Which I Refuse Contemplation   *176*

II

Mississippi   *181*

After Storm   *181*

Watching *Last Year at Marienbad* at Roger Haggerty's House
    in Auburn, Alabama   *182*

Dog Days, Jerusalem   *183*

Ozone   *183*

Turning Thirty, I Contemplate Students Bicycling Home   *184*

Particulars   *185*

Your Death   *186*

The Wake   *187*

III

The Other Side of the House   *191*

Pastoral   *192*

Horse and Tree   *192*

The Breathing, The Endless News   *193*

After Reading *Mickey in the Night Kitchen* for the Third Time
    Before Bed   *193*

Genetic Expedition   *194*

Backyard, 6 a.m.   *195*

IV

Dedication   *199*

Ars Poetica   *199*

Arrow   *200*

Stitches   *201*

In the Museum   *202*

And Counting   *203*

Dialectical Romance   *204*

Medusa   *205*

In a Neutral City   *205*

V

Saints   *209*

Genie's Prayer under the Kitchen Sink   *209*

The Gorge   *211*

Canary   *213*

The Island Women of Paris   *213*

À l'Opéra   *214*

Obbligato   *214*

Lint   *215*

The Royal Workshops   *216*

On the Road to Damascus   *217*

Old Folk's Home, Jerusalem   *218*

MOTHER LOVE (1995)   *221*

An Intact World   *223*

I

Heroes   *227*

II

Primer *231*

Party Dress for a First Born *231*

Persephone, Falling *232*

The Search *232*

Protection *233*

The Narcissus Flower *233*

Persephone Abducted *234*

Statistic: The Witness *234*

Grief: The Council *235*

Mother Love *236*

Breakfast of Champions *237*

Golden Oldie *238*

III

Persephone in Hell *241*

IV

Hades' Pitch *251*

Wiederkehr *251*

Wiring Home *252*

The Bistro Styx *252*

V

Blue Days *257*

Nature's Itinerary *257*

Sonnet in Primary Colors *258*

Demeter Mourning *258*

Exit *259*

Afield *259*

Lost Brilliance *260*

VI

Political *263*

Demeter, Waiting *263*

Lamentations *264*

Teotihuacán *264*

History *265*

Used *265*

Rusks *266*

Missing *266*

Demeter's Prayer to Hades *267*

VII

Her Island *271*

ON THE BUS WITH ROSA PARKS (1999) *277*

CAMEOS *279*

July 1925—Night—Birth—Lake Erie Skyline, 1930—Depression Years—
Homework—Graduation, Grammar School—Painting the Town—Easter
Sunday, 1940—Nightwatch. The Son.

FREEDOM: BIRD'S-EYE VIEW *291*

Singsong *293*

I Cut My Finger Once on Purpose *293*

Parlor *294*

The First Book *295*

Maple Valley Branch Library, 1967 *296*

Freedom: Bird's-Eye View *297*

Testimonial *298*

Dawn Revisited *299*

BLACK ON A SATURDAY NIGHT *301*

My Mother Enters the Work Force *303*

Black on a Saturday Night *303*

The Musician Talks About "Process" *304*

Sunday *305*

The Camel Comes to Us from the Barbarians *307*

The Venus of Willendorf *308*

Incarnation in Phoenix *311*

REVENANT *313*

Best Western Motor Lodge, AAA Approved *315*

Revenant *315*

On Veronica *316*

There Came a Soul *317*

The Peach Orchard *318*

Against Repose *319*

Against Self-Pity *320*

Götterdämmerung   *321*

Ghost Walk   *322*

Lady Freedom Among Us   *324*

For Sophie, Who'll Be in First Grade in the Year 2000   *325*

ON THE BUS WITH ROSA PARKS   *327*

Sit Back, Relax   *329*

"The situation is intolerable"   *329*

Freedom Ride   *330*

Climbing In   *331*

Claudette Colvin Goes to Work   *331*

The Enactment   *333*

Rosa   *334*

QE2. Transatlantic Crossing. Third Day.   *334*

In the Lobby of the Warner Theatre, Washington, D.C.   *335*

The Pond, Porch-View: Six p.m., Early Spring   *336*

AMERICAN SMOOTH (2004)   *339*

FOX TROT FRIDAYS   *343*

All Souls'   *345*

"I have been a stranger in a strange land"   *346*

Fox Trot Fridays   *347*

Ta Ta Cha Cha   *347*

Quick   *348*

Brown   *349*

Fox   *350*

Heart to Heart   *351*

Cozy Apología   *352*

Soprano   *353*

Two for the Montrose Drive-In   *354*

Meditation at Fifty Yards, Moving Target   *356*

American Smooth   *358*

NOT WELCOME HERE   *361*

The Castle Walk   *363*

The Passage   *364*

Noble Sissle's Horn   *371*

Alfonzo Prepares to Go Over the Top   *372*

La Chapelle. 92nd Division. Ted.   *373*

Variation on Reclamation   *374*

The Return of Lieutenant James Reese Europe   *376*

Ripont   *377*

TWELVE CHAIRS   *381*

BLUES IN HALF-TONES, 3/4 TIME   *389*

Chocolate   *391*

Bolero   *391*

Hattie McDaniel Arrives at the Coconut Grove   *392*

Samba Summer   *394*

Blues in Half-Tones, 3/4 Time   *395*

Describe Yourself in Three Words or Less   *396*

The Seven Veils of Salomé   *397*

From Your Valentine   *399*

Rhumba   *400*

The Sisters: Swansong.   *403*

EVENING PRIMROSE   *405*

Evening Primrose   *407*

Reverie in Open Air   *407*

Sic Itur Ad Astra   *408*

Count to Ten and We'll Be There   *409*

Eliza, Age 10, Harlem   *409*

Lullaby   *410*

Driving Through   *411*

Desert Backyard   *412*

Desk Dreams   *413*

Now   *415*

Against Flight   *416*

Looking Up from the Page, I Am
     Reminded of This Mortal Coil   *417*

Notes   419

Acknowledgments   422

Index of Titles and First Lines   427

COLLECTED POEMS

IN THE OLD NEIGHBORHOOD

To pull yourself up by your own roots;
to eat the last meal in your own neighborhood.
—ADRIENNE RICH, "Shooting Script"

Raccoons have invaded the crawl space
of my sister's bridal apartment.
The landlord insists they're squirrels;
squirrels he'll fight, not raccoons—
too ferocious and faggy, licking
their black-gloved paws.

My mother works up a sudsbath
of worries: what if
the corsages are too small,
if the candles
accidentally ignite
the reverend's sleeve?

Father prefers a more
reticent glory. He consoles
his roses—dusts them
with fungicide, spades in
fortified earth. Each summer
he brandishes color
over the neighborhood,
year after year producing
lovelier mutants: these
bruised petticoats, for instance,
or this sudden teacup
blazing empty, its rim
a drunken red smear.

I am indoors, pretending
to read today's paper
as I had been taught
twenty years before:
headlines first,
lead story (continued on A-14),
followed by editorials and

local coverage. Even then
I never finished, snared
between datelines—*Santiago,*
Paris, Dakar—names as
unreal as the future
even now.

My brother rummages upstairs;
I skip to the daily horoscope.
I've read every book in this house,
I know which shelf to go to
to taste crumbling saltines
(*don't eat with your nose in a book!*)
and the gritty slick of sardines,
silted bones of no consequence
disintegrating on the tongue. . . .

That was *Romeo and Juliet*,
strangely enough, and just as odd
stuffed green olives
for a premature attempt at *The Iliad*.
Candy buttons went with Brenda Starr,
Bazooka bubble gum with the Justice
League of America. Fig Newtons
and *King Lear*, bitter lemon as well
for Othello, that desolate
conspicuous soul.
But Macbeth demanded dry bread,
crumbs brushed from a lap
as I staggered off the cushions
contrite, having read far past
my mother's calling.

The rummaging's stopped. Well,
he's found it, whatever it was.
Bee vomit, he said once,
that's all honey is, so that
I could not put my tongue to its
jellied flame without tasting
regurgitated blossoms.

In revenge, I would explicate
the strawberry:

how each select seed
chose to breed in darkness,
the stomach's cauldron
brewing a host of vines
trained to climb and snap
a windpipe shut—then
watched my brother's eyes as
Mom sliced the red hearts into sugar
and left them to build their own
improbable juice.

I fold the crossword away,
walk back to the kitchen where
she's stacked platters high
with chicken and silvery cabbage.
Lean at the sink, listen to her chatter
while the pressure cooker ticks
whole again whole again now.

Out where the maple tree
used to stand
there once was a tent
(official Eagle Scout issue):
inside a young girl
weeping and her brother
twitching with bravado
because their father, troop leader
in the pitched dark,
insisted they'd love it by morning.

(Let me go back to the white rock
on the black lawn, the number
stenciled in negative light.
Let me return to the shadow
of a house moored in moonlight,
gables pitched bright above
the extinguished grass,

and stalk the hushed perimeter,
roses closed around their scent,
azaleas dissembling behind the garage
and the bugeyed pansies
leaning over, inquisitive,
in their picketed beds.

What are these, I'll ask, stooping
to lift the pale leaves, and these?
Weeds, my father mutters
from his pillow. *All weeds*.)

Chink, Chink. Sound made by
a starling the first hot morning
in June, when Dad switched on
the attic fan and nothing
stirred—faraway then
a *chink-chip-shiver*,
whittled breath of a bird
caught in the blades.

We each dropped our books
and ran to identify
the first tragedy of the season:
baby sister run down
or a pebbly toad
the lawn mower had shuffled
into liver canapes—
each of us thinking
At least I'm not the one.
Who could guess it would be
a bird with no song,
no plumage worth stopping for?
Who could think up a solution
this anonymous, a switch
flipped on reverse
to blow the feathers out?

"—tea roses, I'd say, plus
a few carnations—and baby's breath,

of course. Are ferns
too much?" I am back
again, matron of honor,
firstborn daughter nodding *yes*
as I wrap bones and eggshells
into old newspaper for burning,
folding the corners in
properly,
as I had been taught to do.

THE
YELLOW
HOUSE
ON
THE
CORNER

(1980)

I

THIS LIFE

The green lamp flares on the table.
You tell me the same thing
as that one,
asleep, upstairs.
Now I see: the possibilities
are golden dresses in a nutshell.

As a child, I fell in love
with a Japanese woodcut
of a girl gazing at the moon.
I waited with her for her lover.
He came in white breeches and sandals.
He had a goatee—he had

your face, though I didn't know it.
Our lives will be the same—
your lips, swollen from whistling
at danger,
and I a stranger
in this desert,
nursing the tough skins of figs.

THE BIRD FRAU

When the boys came home, everything stopped
the way he left it—her apron, the back stairs,
the sun losing altitude over France
as the birds scared up from the fields,
a whirring curtain of flak—

                    Barmherzigkeit!
her son, her man. She went inside, fed the parakeet,
broke its neck. Spaetzle bubbling on the stove,
windchimes tinkling above the steam, her face
in the hall mirror, bloated, a heart.
Let everything go wild!

Blue jays, crows!
She hung suet from branches, the air quick
around her head with tiny spastic machinery
—starlings, finches—her head a crown of feathers.
She ate less, grew lighter, air tunnelling
through bone, singing

                              a small song.
"Ein Liedchen, Kinder!" The children ran away.
She moved about the yard like an old rag bird.
Still at war, she rose at dawn, watching out
for Rudi, come home on crutches,
the thin legs balancing his atom of life.

ROBERT SCHUMANN, OR:
MUSICAL GENIUS BEGINS WITH AFFLICTION

It began with *A*—years before in a room
with a white piano and lyre-back chairs,
Schumann panted on a whore on a coverlet
and the oboe got its chance . . .

It never stops: the alarm
going off in his head is a cry
in a thicket of its own making.
Cello Concerto in A minor,

Symphony in A, Phantasiestücke,
Concerto for Piano and Orchestra
in A minor, Opus 54: the notes
stack themselves onto the score-sheets

like unfamiliar furniture, the music
pulls higher and higher, and still
each phrase returns to *A*
no chord is safe from *A*

Years before, in a room with delicate chairs,
he was happy. There were no wretched sounds.
He was Adam naked in creation,
starting over as the sky rained apples.

HAPPENSTANCE

When you appeared it was as if
magnets cleared the air.
I had never seen that smile before
or your hair, flying silver. Someone
waving goodbye, she was silver, too.
Of course you didn't see me.
I called softly so you could choose
not to answer—then called again.
You turned in the light, your eyes
seeking your name.

SMALL TOWN

Someone is sitting in the red house.
There is no way of telling who it is, although
the woman, indistinct, in the doorway must know;
and the man in the chestnut tree
who wields the binoculars
does not wish to be seen from the window.

The paint was put there by a previous owner.
The dog in the flower bed
is bound by indiscriminate love,
which is why he does not bark
and why in one of the darkened rooms
someone sits, a crackling vacuum.

The woman wears a pale blue nightgown
and stares vaguely upward. The man,
whose form appears clearly among the leaves,
is not looking at her
so much as she at him,
while away behind the town a farmer
weeps, plowing his fields by night
to avoid being laughed at during the day.

THE SNOW KING

In a far far land where men are men
And women are sun and sky,
The snow king paces. And light throws
A gold patina on the white spaces
Where sparrows lie frozen in hallways.

And he weeps for the sparrows, their clumped feathers:
Where is the summer that lasts forever,
The night as soft as antelope eyes?
The snow king roams the lime-filled spaces,
His cracked heart a slow fire, a garnet.

SIGHTSEEING

Come here, I want to show you something.
I inquired about the church yesterday:

the inner courtyard, also in ruin, has been left
exactly as the villagers found it

after the Allies left. What a consort
of broken dolls! Look, they were mounted

at the four corners of the third floor terrace
and the impact from the cobblestones

snapped off wings and other appendages.
The heads rolled the farthest. Someone

started to pile the limbs together—
from the weight of the pieces, an adult—

a deserter, perhaps, or a distraught priest.
Whoever it was, the job was interrupted,

so to speak, in mid-step: this forearm
could not have fallen so far from its owner

without assistance. The villagers,
come here to give thanks, took one look in

and locked the gates: "A terrible sign . . ."
But all this palaver about symbols and

"the ceremony of innocence drowned" is—
as you and I know—civilization's way

of manufacturing hope. Let's look
at the facts. Forget they are children of angels

and they become childish monsters.
Remember, and an arm gracefully upraised

is raised not in anger but a mockery of gesture.
The hand will hold both of mine. The vulgarity

of life in exemplary size is why
we've come to regard this abandoned

constellation, and why two drunks
would walk all the way crosstown

to look at a bunch of smashed statues.

UPON MEETING DON L. LEE, IN A DREAM

He comes toward me with lashless eyes,
Always moving in the yellow half-shadows.
From his mouth I know he has never made love
To thin white boys in toilet stalls . . .

Among the trees, the black trees,
Women in robes stand, watching. They begin
To chant, stamping their feet in wooden cadences
As they stretch their beaded arms to him;

Moments slip by like worms.
"Seven years ago . . ." he begins; but
I cut him off: "Those years are gone—
What is there now?" He starts to cry; his eyeballs

Burst into flame. I can see caviar
Imbedded like buckshot between his teeth.
His hair falls out in clumps of burned-out wire.
The music grows like branches in the wind.

I lie down, chuckling as the grass curls around me.
He can only stand, fists clenched, and weep
Tears of iodine, while the singers float away,
Rustling on brown paper wings.

"TEACH US TO NUMBER OUR DAYS"

In the old neighborhood, each funeral parlor
is more elaborate than the last.
The alleys smell of cops, pistols bumping their thighs,
each chamber steeled with a slim blue bullet.

Low-rent balconies stacked to the sky.
A boy plays tic-tac-toe on a moon
crossed by TV antennae, dreams

he has swallowed a blue bean.
It takes root in his gut, sprouts
and twines upward, the vines curling
around the sockets and locking them shut.

And this sky, knotting like a dark tie?
The patroller, disinterested, holds all the beans.

August. The mums nod past, each a prickly heart on a sleeve.

NIGGER SONG: AN ODYSSEY

We six pile in, the engine churning ink:
We ride into the night.
Past factories, past graveyards
And the broken eyes of windows, we ride
Into the gray-green nigger night.

We sweep past excavation sites; the pits
Of gravel gleam like mounds of ice.
Weeds clutch at the wheels;
We laugh and swerve away, veering
Into the black entrails of the earth,
The green smoke sizzling on our tongues . . .

In the nigger night, thick with the smell of cabbages,
Nothing can catch us.
Laughter spills like gin from glasses,
And "yeah" we whisper, "yeah"
We croon, "yeah."

II

FIVE ELEPHANTS

are walking towards me.
When morning is still a frozen
tear in the brain, they come
from the east, trunk to tail,
clumsy ballerinas.

How to tell them all evening
I refused consolation? Five umbrellas, five
willows, five bridges and their shadows!
They lift their trunks, hooking the sky
I would rush into, split

pod of quartz and lemon. I could say
they are five memories, but
that would be unfair.
Rather pebbles seeking refuge in the heart.
They move past me. I turn and follow,

and for hours we meet no one else.

GEOMETRY

I prove a theorem and the house expands:
the windows jerk free to hover near the ceiling,
the ceiling floats away with a sigh.

As the walls clear themselves of everything
but transparency, the scent of carnations
leaves with them. I am out in the open

and above the windows have hinged into butterflies,
sunlight glinting where they've intersected.
They are going to some point true and unproven.

CHAMPAGNE

The natives here have given up their backyards
and are happy living where we cannot see them.
No shade! The sky insists upon its blueness,
the baskets their roped ovals.
Gravel blinds us, blurring the road's shoulders.
Figures moving against the corduroyed hills
are not an industry to speak of, just
an alchemy whose yield is pleasure.

Come quickly—a whiff of yeast
means bubbles are forming, trapped
by sugar and air. The specialist who turns
30,000 bottles a day 10° to the right
lines up in a vaulted cellar
for an Italian red at the end of the day.
On either side for as far as we can see,
racks of unmarked bottles lying in cool fever.

Three centuries before in this dim corridor
a monk paused to sip, said it pricked
the tongue like stars. When we emerge
it is as difficult to remember the monk
as it is to see things as they are:
houses waver in the heat, stone walls
blaze. The hurt we feel is delicate—
all for ourselves and all for nothing.

NIGHT WATCH

In this stucco house there is nothing but air.
The Mexican sky shivers toward morning.
I am on the four-star vacation from the wings
Of man to these halls draped in heavy matting
Where lizards hang from light fixtures.
From an invisible courtyard comes
The broken applause of castanets.

Romance may lurk in the land of white orchids,
But no slim-hipped Latin comes for me.
Coated servants scuttle through the halls.
I hear the morning wind around the house
As the light goes out
To the shanties in the mountains.

THE SECRET GARDEN

I was ill, lying on my bed of old papers,
when you came with white rabbits in your arms;
and the doves scattered upwards, flying to mothers,
and the snails sighed under their baggage of stone . . .

Now your tongue grows like celery between us:
Because of our love-cries, cabbage darkens in its nest;
the cauliflower thinks of her pale, plump children
and turns greenish-white in a light like the ocean's.

I was sick, fainting in the smell of teabags,
when you came with tomatoes, a good poetry.
I am being wooed. I am being conquered
by a cliff of limestone that leaves chalk on my breasts.

A SUITE FOR AUGUSTUS

1963

That winter I stopped loving the President
And loved his dying. He smiled
From his frame on the chifferobe
And watched as I reined in each day
Using buttons for rosary beads.

Then tapwater rinsed orange through my underwear.
You moved away, and in tall white buildings
Typed speeches, each word-cluster a satellite,

A stone cherry that arced over the violent bay,
Broadcasting ball games and good will to Cuba . . .

But to me, stretched out under percale,
The cherry blinks sadly: Goodbye, goodbye,
Spinning into space. In this black place
I touch the doorknobs of my knees, begging to open
Me, an erector set, spilled and unpuzzled.

D.C.

1
Roosters corn wooden dentures
pins & thimbles embroidery hoops
greenbacks & silver snuff & silver

brontosaurus bones couched on Smithsonian velvet

2
A bloodless finger pointing to heaven, you say,
is surely no more impossible than this city:
A no man's land, a capital askew,
a postcard framed by imported blossoms—
and now this outrageous cue stick
lying, reflected, on a black table.

3
Leaving his chair under the giant knee-cap,
he prowls the edge of the prune-black water.
Down the lane of clipped trees, a ghost trio
plays Dixie. His slaves have outlived him
in this life, too. Harmonicas breathe in,
the gray palms clap: "De broomstick's jumped, the world's
not wide."

Planning the Perfect Evening

I keep him waiting, tuck in the curtains,
buff my nails (such small pink eggshells).
As if for the last time, I descend the stair.

He stands penguin-stiff in a room
that's so quiet we forget it is there.
Now nothing, not even breath, can come

between us, not even the aroma of punch
and sneakers as we dance the length
of the gymnasium and crepe paper streams

down like cartoon lightning. Ah,
Augustus, where did you learn to samba?
And what is that lump below your cummerbund?

Stardust. The band folds up
resolutely, with plum-dark faces.
The night still chirps. Sixteen cars

caravan to Georgia for a terrace,
beer and tacos. Even this far south
a thin blue ice shackles the moon,

and I'm happy my glass sizzles with stars.
How far away the world! And how hulking
you are, my dear, my sweet black bear!

Augustus Observes the Sunset

July. The conspiracy of colors—
Ketchup, marshmallows, the tub of ice,
Bacon strips floating in pale soup.
The sun, like a dragon spreading its tail,
Burns the blue air to ribbons.

Eastward, the corn swelling in its sockets,
A wall of silence, growing.
What are you doing in your own backyard
Holding your coat in your arms?
There's so much left to do!—You pack.
Above spareribs and snow-puffed potatoes
The sky shakes like a flag.

Wake

Stranded in the middle of the nation like this,
I turn eastward, following rivers.
My heart, shy mulatto, wanders toward
The salt-edged contours of rock and sand
That stretch ahead into darkness:

But you stand in the way, a young boy
Appearing on the bank of the Potomac,
Profile turned to sudden metal
And your shirt-front luminous
Under a thicket of cherry boughs.

You open your mouth as if to say
Tadpoles, pebbles,
Each word a droplet of crème de menthe.
What reaches me is not your words
But your breath, exalted and spearmint.

Back

Three years too late, I'm scholarshipped
to Europe and back.
Four years, a language later, and
your 39th jet lands in Kuwait.
(Down

through columns of khaki and ribbons,
escorted at night by the radiance
of oil fields, you relax at last—
goat milk and scotch, no women, no
maple trees. You think: how far I've come)

This barnstorming that led no closer to you
has stuffed my knees into violets,
buried me in the emerald hearts of leaves.
They are like twenty-mark bills, soft
dollars, they bring me back.

III

BELINDA'S PETITION

(Boston, February 1782)

To the honorable Senate and House
of Representatives of this Country,
new born: I am Belinda, an African,
since the age of twelve a Slave.
I will not take too much of your Time,
but to plead and place my pitiable Life
unto the Fathers of this Nation.

Lately your Countrymen have severed
the Binds of Tyranny. I would hope
you would consider the Same for me,
pure Air being the sole Advantage
of which I can boast in my present Condition.

As to the Accusation that I am Ignorant:
I received Existence on the Banks
of the Rio de Valta. All my Childhood
I expected nothing, if that be Ignorance.
The only Travelers were the Dead who returned
from the Ridge each Evening. How might
I have known of Men with Faces like the Moon,
who would ride toward me steadily for twelve Years?

THE HOUSE SLAVE

The first horn lifts its arm over the dew-lit grass
and in the slave quarters there is a rustling—
children are bundled into aprons, cornbread

and water gourds grabbed, a salt pork breakfast taken.
I watch them driven into the vague before-dawn
while their mistress sleeps like an ivory toothpick

and Massa dreams of asses, rum and slave-funk.
I cannot fall asleep again. At the second horn,
the whip curls across the backs of the laggards—

sometimes my sister's voice, unmistaken, among them.
"Oh! pray," she cries. "Oh! pray!" Those days
I lie on my cot, shivering in the early heat,

and as the fields unfold to whiteness,
and they spill like bees among the fat flowers,
I weep. It is not yet daylight.

DAVID WALKER (1785–1830)

Free to travel, he still couldn't be shown how lucky
he was: *They strip and beat and drag us about*
like rattlesnakes. Home on Brattle Street, he took in the sign
on the door of the slop shop. All day at the counter—
white caps, ale-stained pea coats. Compass needles,
eloquent as tuning forks, shivered, pointing north.
Evenings, the ceiling fan sputtered like a second pulse.
Oh Heaven! I am full!! I can hardly move my pen!!!

On the faith of an eye-wink, pamphlets were stuffed
into trouser pockets. Pamphlets transported
in the coat linings of itinerant seamen, jackets
ringwormed with salt traded drunkenly to pursers
in the Carolinas, pamphlets ripped out, read aloud:
Men of colour, who are also of sense.
Outrage. Incredulity. Uproar in state legislatures.

We are the most wretched, degraded and abject set
of beings that ever lived since the world began.
The jewelled canaries in the lecture halls tittered,
pressed his dark hand between their gloves.
Every half-step was no step at all.

Every morning, the man on the corner strung a fresh
bunch of boots from his shoulders. "I'm happy!" he said.
"I never want to live any better or happier than
when I can get a-plenty of boots and shoes to clean!"

A second edition. A third.
The abolitionist press is *perfectly appalled.*
Humanity, kindness and the fear of the Lord
does not consist in protecting devils. A month—
his person (is that all?) found face-down
in the doorway at Brattle Street,
his frame slighter than friends remembered.

THE ABDUCTION

The bells, the cannons, the houses black with crepe,
all for the great Harrison! The citizenry of Washington
clotted the avenue—I among them, Solomon Northup
from Saratoga Springs, free papers in my pocket, violin
under arm, my new friends Brown and Hamilton by my side.

Why should I have doubted them? The wages were good.
While Brown's tall hat collected pennies at the tent flap,
Hamilton's feet did a jig on a tightrope,
pigs squealed invisibly from the bleachers and I fiddled.

I remember how the windows rattled with each report.
Then the wine, like a pink lake, tipped.
I was lifted—the sky swivelled, clicked into place.

I floated on water I could not drink. Though the pillow
was stone, I climbed no ladders in that sleep.

I woke and found myself alone, in darkness and in chains.

THE TRANSPORT OF SLAVES
FROM MARYLAND TO MISSISSIPPI

(On August 22, 1839, a wagonload of slaves broke their chains, killed two
white men, and would have escaped, had not a slave woman helped the
Negro driver mount his horse and ride for help.)

I don't know if I helped him up
because I thought he was our salvation
or not. Left for dead in the middle
of the road, dust hovering around the body
like a screen of mosquitoes
shimmering in the hushed light.
The skin across his cheekbones
burst open like baked yams—
deliberate, the eyelids came apart—
his eyes were my eyes in a yellower face.
*Death and salvation—*one accommodates the other.
I am no brute. I got feelings.
He might have been a son of mine.

     ᪐

"The Negro Gordon, barely escaping with his life, rode
into the plantation just as his pursuers came into sight.
The neighborhood was rallied and a search begun.
Some of the Negroes had taken to the woods but
were routed, ending this most shocking affray and murder."

     ᪐

Eight miles south of Portsmouth, the last handcuff
broke clean from the skin. The last thing
the driver saw were the trees, improbable as broccoli,
before he was clubbed from behind. Sixty slaves
poured off the wagon, smelly, half-numb, free.

Baggage man Petit rushed in with his whip.
Some nigger's laid on another one's leg, he thought
before he saw they were loose. *Hold it!* he yelled;

but not even the wenches stopped. To his right
Atkins dropped under a crown of clubs. They didn't
even flinch. *Wait. You ain't supposed to act this way.*

PAMELA

"*. . . the hour was come when the man must act, or forever be a slave.*"

> At two, the barnyard settled
> into fierce silence—anvil,
> water pump glinted
> as though everything waited
> for the first step.
> She stepped
> into the open. The wind
> lifted—behind her,
> fields spread their sails.

There really is a star up there and moss on the trees. She
discovered if she kept a steady pace, she could walk forever.
The idea pleased her, and she hummed a hymn to herself—
Peach Point, Silk Hope, Beaver Bend. It seemed that the further
north she went, the freer she became. The stars were plates
for good meat; if she reached, they flashed and became coins.

> White quiet. Night pushed over the hill.
> The woods hiss with cockleburs,
> each a small woolly head.
> She feels old, older
> than these friendly shadows
> who, like the squirrels, don't come too near.
> Knee-deep in muscadine, she watches them coming,
> snapping the brush. They are
> smiling, rifles crossed on their chests.

SOMEONE'S BLOOD

I stood at 6 a.m. on the wharf,
thinking: *This is Independence, Missouri.*
I am to stay here. The boat goes on to New Orleans.
My life seemed minutes old, and here it was ending.

I was silent, although she clasped me
and asked forgiveness for giving me life.
As the sun broke the water into a thousand needles
tipped with the blood from someone's finger,

the boat came gently apart from the wharf.
I watched till her face could not distinguish itself
from that shadow floated on broken sunlight.
I stood there. I could not help her. I forgive.

CHOLERA

At the outset, hysteria.
Destruction, the conjurers intoned.
Some dragged themselves off at night
to die in the swamp, to lie down
with the voices of mud and silk.

I know moonrise, I know starrise

Against orders
the well and almost-well were assembled
and marched into the wood. When
a dry open place was found, halted.
The very weak got a piece of board
and fires were built, though the evening was warm.
Said the doctor, You'll live.

I walk in de moonlight, I walk in de starlight

Who could say but that it wasn't anger
had to come out somehow? Pocketed filth.
The pouring-away of pints of pale fluid.

I'll walk in de graveyard, I'll walk through de graveyard

Movement, dark and silken.
The dry-skinned conjurers circling the fire.
Here is pain, they whispered, and it is all ours.
Who would want to resist them?
By camplight their faces had taken on
the frail finality of ash.

I'll lie in de grave and stretch out my arms

Well,
that was too much for the doctor.
Strip 'em! he ordered. And they
were slicked down with bacon fat and
superstition strapped from them
to the beat of the tam-tam. Those strong enough
rose up too, and wailed as they leapt.
It was a dance of unusual ferocity.

THE SLAVE'S CRITIQUE OF PRACTICAL REASON

Ain't got a reason
to run away—
leastways, not one
would save my life.
So I scoop speculation
into a hopsack.
I scoop fluff till
the ground rears white
and I'm the only dark
spot in the sky.

All day the children
sit in the weeds
to wait out the heat
with the rattlers.
All day Our Lady
of the Milk-Tooth
attends them
while I, the Owl
of the Broken Spirit
keep dipping and
thinking up tunes
that fly off quick
as they hit
the air. As far
as I can see,

it's hotter in heaven
than in the cool
cool earth. I know
'cause I've been there,
a stony mote
circling the mindless
blue, dropping rows
of little clouds,
no-good reasons
for sale.

KENTUCKY, 1833

It is Sunday, day of roughhousing. We are let out in the woods. The young
boys wrestle and butt their heads together like sheep—a circle forms; claps
and shouts fill the air. The women, brown and glossy, gather round the banjo
player, or simply lie in the sun, legs and aprons folded. The weather's an odd
monkey—any other day he's on our backs, his cotton eye everywhere; today
the light sifts down like the finest cornmeal, coating our hands and arms with
a dust. God's dust, old woman Acker says. She's the only one who could read
to us from the Bible, before Massa forbade it. On Sundays, something hangs

in the air, a hallelujah, a skitter of brass, but we can't call it by name and it disappears.

Then Massa and his gentlemen friends come to bet on the boys. They guffaw and shout, taking sides, red-faced on the edge of the boxing ring. There is more kicking, butting, and scuffling—the winner gets a dram of whiskey if he can drink it all in one swig without choking.

Jason is bucking and prancing about—Massa said his name reminded him of some sailor, a hero who crossed an ocean, looking for a golden cotton field. Jason thinks he's been born to great things—a suit with gold threads, vest and all. Now the winner is sprawled out under a tree and the sun, that weary tambourine, hesitates at the rim of the sky's green light. It's a crazy feeling that carries through the night; as if the sky were an omen we could not understand, the book that, if we could read, would change our lives.

IV

ADOLESCENCE—I

In water-heavy nights behind grandmother's porch
We knelt in the tickling grasses and whispered:
Linda's face hung before us, pale as a pecan,
And it grew wise as she said:
    "A boy's lips are soft,
    As soft as baby's skin."
The air closed over her words.
A firefly whirred near my ear, and in the distance
I could hear streetlamps ping
Into miniature suns
Against a feathery sky.

ADOLESCENCE—II

Although it is night, I sit in the bathroom, waiting.
Sweat prickles behind my knees, the baby-breasts are alert.
Venetian blinds slice up the moon; the tiles quiver in pale strips.

Then they come, the three seal men with eyes as round
As dinner plates and eyelashes like sharpened tines.
They bring the scent of licorice. One sits in the washbowl,

One on the bathtub edge; one leans against the door.
"Can you feel it yet?" they whisper.
I don't know what to say, again. They chuckle,

Patting their sleek bodies with their hands.
"Well, maybe next time." And they rise,
Glittering like pools of ink under moonlight,

And vanish. I clutch at the ragged holes
They leave behind, here at the edge of darkness.
Night rests like a ball of fur on my tongue.

ADOLESCENCE—III

With Dad gone, Mom and I worked
The dusky rows of tomatoes.
As they glowed orange in sunlight
And rotted in shadow, I too
Grew orange and softer, swelling out
Starched cotton slips.

The texture of twilight made me think of
Lengths of Dotted Swiss. In my room
I wrapped scarred knees in dresses
That once went to big-band dances;
I baptized my earlobes with rosewater.
Along the window-sill, the lipstick stubs
Glittered in their steel shells.

Looking out at the rows of clay
And chicken manure, I dreamed how it would happen:
He would meet me by the blue spruce,
A carnation over his heart, saying,
"I have come for you, Madam;
I have loved you in my dreams."
At his touch, the scabs would fall away.
Over his shoulder, I see my father coming toward us:
He carries his tears in a bowl,
And blood hangs in the pine-soaked air.

THE BOAST

At the dinner table, before the baked eggplant,
you tell the story of your friend, Ira,
how he kept a three-foot piranha in his basement.
"It was this long," you say, extending your arms,
"And it was striped, with silver scales and blue shadows."

The man with purple eyes lifts his eyebrows;
you laugh at his joke about the lady

in the sausage suit, your toes find his
under the table, and he is yours.

Evening expires in a yawn of stars.
But on the walk home,
when he pulls you into the hedges,
and the black tongues of leaves flutter,
and those boogy-man eyes glitter,
there won't be time for coming back
with lies, with lies.

THE KADAVA KUMBIS DEVISE A WAY
TO MARRY FOR LOVE

I will marry this clump of flowers
and throw it into the well!

There is no comfort in poverty.
"Better," they say, "to give yourself

to the soil under your feet
than to a man without jewels.

Who can feast off wind?"
So bring the gongs and the

old women—let us mourn
the loss of my youthful husband!

Where his frail hands paused
breath lingered, so that I am now

restless, a perfumed fan.
Who has suffered once

is not subject to pride.
I will marry again—perhaps to

that ragged man on the hill,
watching from a respectful distance.

SPY

She walked alone, as she did every morning.
Hers the narrow sidewalk, the corroded lamppost.
Larks thrilled the apricot air. Barbed crucifixes

Against the sky, the haloes of mist around streetlamps—
They reminded her of Jesus on a gilded altar
And Mama in a blue apron, praying.

Where were the oily midnights of depravity?
A woman of hard edges, blonde with dark armpits—
Where was she but always coming in from the cold?

FIRST KISS

And it was almost a boy who undid
the double sadness I'd sealed away.
He built a house in a meadow
no one stopped to admire,

and wore wrong clothes. Nothing
seemed to get in his way.
I promised him anything
if he would go. He smiled

and left. How
to re-create his motives,
irretrievable

as a gasp? Where else
to find him, counter-rising
in me, almost a boy. . . .

THEN CAME FLOWERS

I should have known if you gave me flowers
They would be chrysanthemums.
The white spikes singed my fingers.
I cried out; they spilled from the green tissue
And spread at my feet in a pool of soft fire.

If I begged you to stay, what good would it do me?
In the bed, you would lay the flowers between us.
I will pick them up later, arrange them with pincers.
All night from the bureau they'll watch me, their
Plumage as proud, as cocky as firecrackers.

PEARLS

You have broken the path of the dragonfly
who visits my patio at the hour when
the sky has nearly forgotten the sun.
You have come to tell me
how happy we are, but I know
what you would and would not do
to make us happy. For example this necklace
before me: white eyes,
a noose of guileless tears.

NEXUS

I wrote stubbornly into the evening.
At the window, a giant praying mantis
rubbed his monkey wrench head against the glass,
begging vacantly with pale eyes;

and the commas leapt at me like worms
or miniature scythes blackened with age.
The praying mantis screeched louder,
his ragged jaws opening onto formlessness.

I walked outside;
the grass hissed at my heels.
Up ahead in the lapping darkness
he wobbled, magnified and absurdly green,
a brontosaurus, a poet.

V

NOTES FROM A TUNISIAN JOURNAL

This nutmeg stick of a boy in loose trousers!
Little coffee pots in the coals, a mint on the tongue.

The camels stand in all their vague beauty—
at night they fold up like pale accordions.

All the hedges are singing with yellow birds!
A boy runs by with lemons in his hands.

Food's perfume, breath is nourishment.
The stars crumble, salt above eucalyptus fields.

THE SAHARA BUS TRIP

I. *Departure*

Roofless houses, cartons of chalk,
catch the sky in their mirrors of air.
Intake of breath. Crisp
trees hung with sour oranges.
Hunched in the unnatural light, you wait
for the driver to start this bus forward.
Dust scatters in the pus-filled eyes
of children running after us, waving.
How small they are! They are getting smaller.

II. *The Discovery of Oranges*

At night they quiver imperceptibly until
the leaves rustle; their perforated skins
give off a faint heat.
Only the Arab knows the heart of the orange:
she tears herself apart to give us relief.
We spend 200 milliemes for a bag of oranges
so sweet our tongues lie dreaming in the juice.

III. *The Salt Sea*

If, at the end of the Atlantic,
Columbus had found only an absence of water,
this English tourist would have been there
to capture that void with a wide-angle lens.
Here, the wind blows from nowhere to nowhere
across a plain transformed by salt
into a vision of light. One bug,
black and white, dusted with salt, crawls
among orange peels that flare up like
brittle flowers. *You could not live here,*
he says. *It is not so astonishing,*
close your mouths.

IV. *The Discovery of Sandroses*

Each inconsolable thought sprouts
a tear of salt which blossoms,
sharpens into a razored petal.
Now we have a bouquet of stone roses.
The bedouins are hawking the new miracle,
600 milliemes, a few francs!
You buy me a large one.
By the roadside, the boys pose with foxes—
those diseased bastard eyes, those crumbling smiles.

V. *Hotel Nefta*

We disembark, the bus wheezing
like a punctured furnace.
The Englishman has set his tripod up
and is shooting the green interference of palms.
It is tricky light. Tomorrow the trip back,
our fingers exhaling small, tangy breaths.
What a light-hearted whistle you have!
It reminds me of water—so far-away,
so clear, it must come from the sky.

FOR KAZUKO

The bolero, silk-tassled, the fuchsia
scarf come off: all that black hair

for the asking! You are unbraiding
small braids, your face full

behind a curtain of dark breath. Why
am I surprised when your lids emerge

from the fragrant paint? Now the couch
is baring its red throat, and now

you must understand me: your breasts,
so tiny, wound—or more precisely, echo

all the breasts which cannot swell, which
we prefer. I would like to lose myself

in those hushing thighs; but
sadness is not enough. A phallus

walks your dreams, Kazuko, lovely and
unidentified. Here is an anthology of wishes:

if fucking were graceful, desire an alibi.

BEAUTY AND THE BEAST

Darling, the plates have been cleared away,
the servants are in their quarters.
What lies will we lie down with tonight?
The rabbit pounding in your heart, my

child legs, pale from a life of petticoats?
My father would not have had it otherwise
when he trudged the road home with our souvenirs.
You are so handsome it eats my heart away . . .

Beast, when you lay stupid with grief
at my feet, I was too young to see anything
die. Outside, the roses are folding
lip upon red lip. I miss my sisters—

they are standing before their clouded mirrors.
Gray animals are circling under the windows.
Sisters, don't you see what will snatch you up—
the expected, the handsome, the one who needs us?

HIS SHIRT

does not show his
true colors. Ice-

blue and of stuff
so common

anyone
could have bought it,

his shirt
is known only

to me, and only
at certain times

of the day.
At dawn

it is a flag
in the middle

of a square
waiting to catch

chill light.
Unbuttoned, it's

a sail surprised
by boundless joy.

In candlelight at turns
a penitent's

scarf or beggar's
fleece, his shirt is

inapproachable.
It is the very shape

and tint
of desire

and could be mistaken
for something quite

fragile and
ordinary.

GREAT UNCLE BEEFHEART

It was not as if he didn't try
to tell us: first he claimed
the velvet armchair, then the sun
on the carpet before it. Silence,
too, he claimed, although
we tried to spoil it with humming
and children's games. There was
that much charm left in the world.

It was not as if he didn't want
to believe us: he kept himself
neat. Behind his head, the anti-
macassar darkened, surrendered
the fragrance of bergamot.
Things creaked when he touched

them, so he stopped that, too.
He called us "dear little bugs,"

and it was not as if he
acted strange, though our mother
told her mother once
at least his heart was bigger
than any other man's.
That's when we called him
Great Uncle Beefheart; and it was not
as if he listened: he just

walked outdoors. Sunflowers,
wildly prosperous, took
the daylight and shook it
until our vision ran.
We found him in his shirtsleeves
in the onion patch, shivering
as he cried *I can't go back in
there, I ain't wearing no clothes.*

THE SON

All the toothy Fräuleins are left behind:
blood machinery pumps the distance between you.
At the moment the landing gear
groans into the belly,
Mama's outside the window
in her shawl and her seed pearls.
She comes for help—your brother's
knocked down while restraining an inmate
and the family's counting on you . . .

A year ago Wagner sang you down the Rhine.
You stood in the failing light, certain
the Lorelei would toss you her comb.
Life could not bank and drop

you on the coal shores of Pittsburgh,
the house by factory light opening
its reluctant arms to boarders.

CORDUROY ROAD

We strike camp on that portion of road completed
during the day. The strip of sky above me
darkens: this afternoon when it lurched into view
I felt air swoop down, and breathed it in.

Instruction:
Avoiding bogs and unduly rough terrain
Clear a track two rods wide
From Prairie du Chien to Fort Howard at Green Bay.

Today Carlton devised an interesting pastime.
From each trunk the axe has razed
a startled, upturned face awaits
refinement by the penknife:
The Jester. The Statesman. The Sot. The Maiden.

The symbol of motion is static, finite,
And kills by the coachload. Chances of perishing
On the road are ten to one, calculated
According to the following table of casualties:
 1. By horses running away.
 2. By overturning.
 3. By drowning.
 4. By murder.
 5. By explosion.

Whenever a tree is felled, I think of a thousand blankets
ripped into sparks, or that the stillness itself
has been found and torn open with bare hands.
What prevails a man to hazard his person in the Wisconsin Forests
is closer to contrition than anything: the wild honey
blazing from outstretched palms, a skunk bagged and eaten in tears.

Ö

Shape the lips to an *o*, say *a*.
That's *island*.

One word of Swedish has changed the whole neighborhood.
When I look up, the yellow house on the corner
is a galleon stranded in flowers. Around it

the wind. Even the high roar of a leaf-mulcher
could be the horn-blast from a ship
as it skirts the misted shoals.

We don't need much more to keep things going.
Families complete themselves
and refuse to budge from the present,
the present extends its glass forehead to sea
(backyard breezes, scattered cardinals)

and if, one evening, the house on the corner
took off over the marshland,
neither I nor my neighbor
would be amazed. Sometimes

a word is found so right it trembles
at the slightest explanation.
You start out with one thing, end
up with another, and nothing's
like it used to be, not even the future.

MUSEUM

(1983)

for nobody
who made us possible

I

THE HILL HAS SOMETHING TO SAY

Here lies
Ike Tell:
Heathen.
No chance of Heaven,
No fear of Hell.

—tombstone near
Weimar, Texas

THE FISH IN THE STONE

The fish in the stone
would like to fall
back into the sea.

He is weary
of analysis, the small
predictable truths.
He is weary of waiting
in the open,
his profile stamped
by a white light.

In the ocean the silence
moves and moves

and so much is unnecessary!
Patient, he drifts
until the moment comes
to cast his
skeletal blossom.

The fish in the stone
knows to fail is
to do the living
a favor.

He knows why the ant
engineers a gangster's
funeral, garish
and perfectly amber.
He knows why the scientist
in secret delight
strokes the fern's
voluptuous braille.

THE ANTS OF ARGOS

There stood the citadel—nothing left.
We climbed it anyway, if for no other reason
than to say we'd been someplace
where earth and air had been quietly
rearranged. Nothing was left

but you and me, standing above the small
and empty harbor flashing blue.
Around us wild thyme ached in mauve
and sun-baked stones fumed piquant
wherever shepherd boys had pissed

to hear them sizzle. Even the ants,
marching skyward, had been in Corinth.

PITHOS

Climb
into a jar
and live
for a while.

Chill earth.
No stars
in this stone
sky.

You have ceased
to ache.

Your spine is
a flower.

NESTOR'S BATHTUB

As usual, legend got it all
wrong: Nestor's wife was the one
to crouch under
jug upon jug of fragrant water poured
until the small room steamed.
But where was Nestor—
on his throne before the hearth,
counting the jars of oil
in storeroom 34, or
at the Trojan wars
while his wife with her white hands
scraped the dirt from a lover's back
with a bronze scalpel?

Legend, as usual, doesn't
say. But this heap of limestone
blocks—look how they fell, blasted
by the force of olive oil
exploding in the pot, look
at the pattern left in stucco
from the wooden columns, sixty
flutings, look at the shards
scattered in the hall where
jars spilled from the second floor,
oil spreading in flames
to the lady's throne.

For the sake of legend only the tub
stands, tiny and voluptuous
as a gravy dish.
And the blackened remains of ivory
combs and 2,853 tall-stemmed
drinking cups in the pantry—
these, too, survived
when the clay pots screamed
and stones sprang their sockets
and the olive trees grew into the hill.

THE HILL HAS SOMETHING TO SAY

but isn't talking.
Instead the valley groans as the wind,
amphoric,
hoots its one bad note.
Halfway up, we stop to peek
through smudged pine: this is Europe
and its green terraces.

and takes its time.
What's left
to climb's inside us,
earth rising, stupified.

: it's not all in the books
(but maps don't lie).
The hill has a right
to stand here, one knob
in the coiled spine of a peasant
who, forgetting to flee, simply
lay down forever.

bootstrap and spur
harrow and pitchfork
a bugle a sandal
clay head of a pipe

(For all we know
the wind's inside us, pacing
our lungs. For all we know
it's spring and the ground

moistens as raped maids break
to blossom. What's invisible
sings, and we bear witness.)

᷍

if we would listen! Underfoot
slow weight, Scavenger Time,
and the little old woman
who lives there still.

THE COPPER BEECH

Aristocrat among patriarchs, this
noble mutation is the best
specimen of Rococo

in the park of the castle
at Erpenberg.
The widely-traveled Baroness

returned
from a South American expedition
with any number of plants and a few

horticultural innovations.
This trailing beech became Erpenberg's
tree of grief, their

melancholy individualist,
the park philosopher.
Eight meters above lawn

the tousled crown
rises, her many plaited branches falling
like green water

earthwards, a cascade of leaves.
The aesthetic principles
of the period: branches

pruned late to heal
into knots, proud flesh ascending
the trunk:

living architecture.

TOU WAN SPEAKS TO HER HUSBAND, LIU SHENG

I will build you a house
of limited chambers
but it shall last
forever: four rooms
hewn in the side of stone
for you, my
only conqueror.

In the south room all
you will need for the journey
—a chariot, a
dozen horses—
opposite,

a figurine household
poised in servitude
and two bronze jugs, worth more
than a family pays in taxes
for the privilege to stay
alive, a year, together . . .

but you're bored.
Straight ahead then, the hall
leading to you, my

constant
emperor. Here
when the stench of your
own diminishing
drives you to air (but

you will find none), here
an incense burner
in the form of the mountain
around you, where hunters pursue
the sacred animal
and the peaks are drenched
in sun.

For those times
in your niche when darkness
oppresses, I will set you
a lamp. (And a statue
of the palace girl you most
frequently coveted.)

And for your body,
two thousand jade wafers
with gold thread puzzled
to a brilliant envelope,
a suit to keep
the shape of your death—

when you are long light and clouds
over the earth, just as the legends prophesy.

CATHERINE OF ALEXANDRIA

Deprived of learning and
    the chance to travel,
no wonder sainthood
    came as a voice

in your bed—
    and what went on
each night was fit
    for nobody's ears

but Jesus'. His
    breath of a lily.
His spiraling
    pain. Each morning

the nightshirt bunched
    above your waist—
a kept promise,
    a ring of milk.

CATHERINE OF SIENA

You walked the length of Italy
to find someone to talk to.
You struck the boulder at the roadside
since fate has doors everywhere.
Under the star-washed dome
of heaven, warm and dark

as the woolens stacked on cedar
shelves back home in your
father's shop, you prayed
until tears streaked the sky.
No one stumbled across your path.
No one unpried your fists as you slept.

RECEIVING THE STIGMATA

There is a way to enter a field
empty-handed, your shoulder
behind you and air tightening.

The kite comes by itself,
a spirit on a fluttering string.

Back when people died for
the smallest reasons, there was
always a field to walk into.
Simple men fell to their knees
below the radiant crucifix
and held out their palms

in relief. Go into the field
and it will reward. Grace

is a string growing straight
from the hand. Is
the hatchet's shadow on the
rippling green.

BOCCACCIO: THE PLAGUE YEARS

Even at night the air rang and rang.
Through the thick swirled glass
he watched the priests sweep past
in their peaked hoods, collecting death.
On each stoop a dish burning sweet
clotted smoke. He closed his eyes
to hear the slap
of flesh onto flesh, a
liquid crack like a grape
as it breaks on the tongue.

As a boy he had slipped
along the same streets, in love with
he didn't know whom. O the
reeded sonatinas and torch
flick on the chill slick sides
of the bridge and steam
rising in plumes

from the slaughterhouse vents—
twenty years.

Rolling out of the light
he leaned his cheek
against the rows of bound leather:
cool water. Fiammetta!
He had described her
a hundred ways; each time
she had proven unfaithful. If only
he could crack this city in two
so the moon would scour
the wormed streets clean! Or
walk away from it all, simply
falling in love again. . . .

FIAMMETTA BREAKS HER PEACE

I've watched them, mother, and I know
the signs. The first day, rigor.
Staggering like drunks, they
ram the room's sharp edges
with the most delicate bodily parts
and feel no pain. Unable
to sleep, they shiver beneath
all the quilts in the house,
panic gnawing a silver path to the brain.

Day two is fever, the bright
stream clogged, eyes rodent
red. No one weeps anymore; just
waits, for appear they must—
in the armpits, at the groin—
hard, blackened apples.
Then, at least, there is certainty,
an odd kind of relief;
a cross comes on the door.

A few worthy citizens gather possessions
around them and spend time
with fine foods, wine and music
behind closed drapes. Having left
the world already, they are surprised
when the world finds them again.
Still others carouse from tavern
to tavern, doing exactly as they please. . . .

And to think he wanted me
beautiful! To be his fresh air
and my breasts two soft
spiced promises. *Stand still*, he said
once, *and let me admire you.*

All is infection, mother—and avarice,
and self-pity, and fear!
We shall sit quietly in this room,
and I think we'll be spared.

II

IN THE BULRUSH

When the morning gather the rainbow,
want you to know I'm a rainbow, too.

—BOB MARLEY

NOVEMBER FOR BEGINNERS

Snow would be the easy
way out—that softening
sky like a sigh of relief
at finally being allowed
to yield. No dice.
We stack twigs for burning
in glistening patches
but the rain won't give.

So we wait, breeding
mood, making music
of decline. We sit down
in the smell of the past
and rise in a light
that is already leaving.
We ache in secret,
memorizing

a gloomy line
or two of German.
When spring comes
we promise to act
the fool. Pour,
rain! Sail, wind,
with your cargo of zithers!

READING HÖLDERLIN ON THE PATIO
WITH THE AID OF A DICTIONARY

One by one, the words
give themselves
up, white flags dispatched
from a silent camp.

When had my shyness returned?

This evening, the sky refused
to lie down. The sun crouched
behind leaves, but the trees
had long since walked away.
The meaning that surfaces

comes to me aslant and
I go to meet it, stepping
out of my body
word for word, until I am

everything at once: the perfume
of the world in which
I go under,
a skindiver
remembering air.

SHAKESPEARE SAY

He drums the piano wood,
crowing.

Champion Jack in love
and in debt,
in a tan walking suit
with a flag on the pocket,
with a red eye
for women, with a
diamond-studded
ear, with sand
in a mouthful of mush—

poor me
poor me
I keep on drifting
like a ship out
on the sea

That afternoon two students
from the Akademie
showed him the town.
Munich was misbehaving,
whipping
his ass to ice
while his shoes
soaked through. His guides
pointed at a clock
in a blue-tiled house.
And tonight

every song he sings
is written by Shakespeare
and his mother-in-law.
I love you, baby,
but it don't mean
a goddam thing.
In trouble
with every woman he's
ever known, all of them
ugly—skinny legs, lie gap
waiting behind the lips
to suck him in.

Going down slow
crooning *Shakespeare say*
man must be
careful what he kiss
when he drunk,
going down
for the third set
past the stragglers
at the bar,
the bourbon in his hand
some bitch's cold
wet heart,
the whole joint

stinking on beer;
in love and winning
now, so even the mistakes
sound like jazz,
poor me, moaning
so no one hears:

my home's in Louisiana,
my voice is wrong,
I'm broke and can't hold
my piss;
my mother told me
there'd be days like this.

THREE DAYS OF FOREST, A RIVER, FREE

The dogs have nothing better
to do than bark; duty's whistle
slings a bright cord
around their throats.
I'll stand here all night
if need be, no more real
than a tree when no moon shines.

The terror of waking is a trust
drawn out unbearably
until nothing, not even love,
makes it easier, and yet
I love this life:

three days of forest,
the mute riot of leaves.

Who can point out a smell
but a dog? The way is free
to the river. Tell me,
Lord, how it feels
to burst out like a rose.

Blood rises in my head—
I'm there.
Faint tongue, dry fear,
I think I lost you to the dogs,
so far off now they're no
more than a chain of bells
ringing darkly, underground.

BANNEKER

What did he do except lie
under a pear tree, wrapped in
a great cloak, and meditate
on the heavenly bodies?
Venerable, the good people of Baltimore
whispered, shocked and more than
a little afraid. After all it was said
he took to strong drink.
Why else would he stay out
under the stars all night
and why hadn't he married?

But who would want him! Neither
Ethiopian nor English, neither
lucky nor crazy, a capacious bird
humming as he penned in his mind
another enflamed letter
to President Jefferson— he imagined
the reply, polite and rhetorical.
Those who had been to Philadelphia
reported the statue
of Benjamin Franklin
before the library

his very size and likeness.
A wife? No, thank you.
At dawn he milked
the cows, then went inside

and put on a pot to stew
while he slept. The clock
he whittled as a boy
still ran. Neighbors
woke him up
with warm bread and quilts.
At nightfall he took out

his rifle— a white-maned
figure stalking the darkened
breast of the Union— and
shot at the stars, and by chance
one went out. Had he killed?
I assure thee, my dear Sir!
Lowering his eyes to fields
sweet with the rot of spring, he could see
a government's domed city
rising from the morass and spreading
in a spiral of lights. . . .

IN THE BULRUSH

Cut a cane that once
grew in the river.
Lean on it. Weigh

a stone in your hands
and put it down again.
Watch it moss over.

Strike the stone
to see if it's thinking
of water.

DELFT

Flat, with variations. Not
the table but the cloth.
As if a continent
raging westward, staggered
at the sight of
so much water, sky
on curdling sky.

Wherever I walk
the earth's soft
mouth suckles.
These clumps of beeches,
glazed trunks
green with age.
Each brick house the original
oven, fired to stay
incipient mold,

while in the hour
of least resolve
the starched sheets
scratch the insomniac wife
to bravado. *At least*,
she whispers,

we dine in style.
And our sceneries
please. We may be standing
on a porch
open to the world
but the house behind us
is sinking.

IKE

Grew hair for fun.
Found a mouth harp.
Scared away the bees.

The creek and the ford
Built step by step.
Sassy finch: kept time
To his creaking knee.

Up the hill fine
Families benched
And wailing. Organ
Panting, a diseased
Lung.

Marched outback.
Shot a cottonmouth.

Heard it twitch
The whole night long.

AGOSTA THE WINGED MAN
AND RASHA THE BLACK DOVE

Schad paced the length of his studio
and stopped at the wall,
                              staring
at a blank space. Behind him
the clang and hum of Hardenbergstrasse, its
automobiles and organ grinders.
                              Quarter to five.
His eyes traveled
to the plaster scrollwork
on the ceiling. Did *that*
                              hold back heaven?
He could not leave his skin—once

he'd painted himself in a new one,
silk green, worn
like a shirt.
                    He thought
of Rasha, so far from Madagascar,
turning slowly in place as
the boa constrictor
coiled counterwise its
                              heavy love. How
the spectators gawked, exhaling
beer and sour herring sighs.
When the tent lights dimmed,
Rasha went back to her trailer and plucked
a chicken for dinner.
                              The canvas,

not his eye, was merciless.
He remembered Katja the Russian
aristocrat, late
for every sitting,
                    still fleeing
the October Revolution—
how she clutched her sides
and said not
                    one word. Whereas Agosta
(the doorbell rang)
was always on time, lip curled
as he spoke in wonder of women
                                        trailing
backstage to offer him
the consummate bloom of their lust.

Schad would place him
on a throne, a white sheet tucked
over his loins, the black suit jacket
thrown off like a cloak.
Agosta had told him
                    of the medical students
at the Charité,
that chill arena

where he perched on
a cot, his torso
exposed, its crests and fins
a colony of birds, trying
to get out . . .
            and the students,
lumps caught
in their throats, taking notes.

Ah, Rasha's
            foot on the stair.
She moved slowly, as if she carried
the snake around her body
always.
            Once
she brought fresh eggs into
the studio, flecked and
warm as breath.
                Agosta in
classical drapery, then,
and Rasha at his feet.
Without passion. Not
the canvas
            but their gaze,
            so calm,
was merciless.

AT THE GERMAN WRITERS CONFERENCE
IN MUNICH

In the large hall of the Hofbräuhaus
above the heads of the members
of the board, taut and white
as skin (not mine),
tacked across a tapestry
this banner:

Association of German
Writers in the Union of Print
and Papercraft.

Below it some flowers,
typical medieval,
and a maiden's feet
under a printed silk gown.
The tapestry pokes out

all over: a woman
in a green kerchief,
a king with a scepter and
crown puffed like a soufflé;
an ash-blonde princess
by birthright permitted
to bare her crinklets
to sun and smoke. Then another
lady-in-waiting, this time
in a white kerchief
and a white horse craning
to observe the royal party.

At the bottom strip of needlework
four flat bread loaves.
Far in the eaves
two doves signify
a union endorsed
by God and the Church.
Further, green hills
rolling with pine.

Above them all a banner
unfurled and inscribed
in Latin. Maybe it says
Association of Tapestrers
in the Union of Wives
and Jewish Dyers.
No one's feet are visible
but those dainty shoes

beneath the printed silk
that first caught my eye,
and the grotesquely bent
fetlock-to-ivory hoof
of the horse. And both
are in flowers.

III

MY FATHER'S TELESCOPE

Then I went an' stood up on some high ol' lonesome hill
An' looked down on the house where I used to live

—BESSIE SMITH

GRAPE SHERBET

The day? Memorial.
After the grill
Dad appears with his masterpiece—
swirled snow, gelled light.
We cheer. The recipe's
a secret and he fights
a smile, his cap turned up
so the bib resembles a duck.

That morning we galloped
through the grassed-over mounds
and named each stone
for a lost milk tooth. Each dollop
of sherbet, later,
is a miracle,
like salt on a melon that makes it sweeter.

Everyone agrees—it's wonderful!
It's just how we imagined lavender
would taste. The diabetic grandmother
stares from the porch,
a torch
of pure refusal.

We thought no one was lying
there under our feet,
we thought it
was a joke. I've been trying
to remember the taste,
but it doesn't exist.
Now I see why
you bothered,
father.

ROSES

It's time you learned something.
Halfway outdoors
he pauses, the flat dark fury of
his jaw, one eye, a shoulder in torn
blue cloth, the pruning shears
a mammoth claw resting
between meals.

          I scramble
up, terrified and down
the drive, the gravel's
brittle froth
and stand completely
helpless as he parts
a thousand pinkish eyelids
to find the beetles nested
at the root, teeming
disease.

They came from Japan, 1961.
They were nothing like the locusts
we hadn't noticed until they
were gone, the husks
sheer tuxedos
snagged on bark, the rafters,
the dying bayberry.

          It's easy—
pop them between your nails.
In the tool shed's populous
shadows, I hold the Mason jar instead
with both hands as he shakes
the flowers above
the kerosene which is shivering now
like the ocean I have never seen . . .

and I bear on a tray indoors
the inculpable, blushing prize.

SUNDAY NIGHT AT GRANDFATHER'S

He liked to joke and all of his jokes were practical.
The bent thumb jiggling between two ribs, his
Faked and drunken swoon. We tipped by and
He caught us, grandfather's right, right
Up to the cliff of his pure white
Shirt, real Fruit-of-the-
Loom. We shrieked and
He cackled like
A living
Ghost.

He hated Billy the parakeet, mean as half-baked sin.
He hated church-going women and the radio turned
Up loud. His favorite son, called Billy
Too, had flown the coop although
Each year he visited, each
Time from a different
City, gold
Tooth and
Drunk.

Then out came the cherry soda and potato chips and pretzels.
Grandma humming hymns and rocking in the back bedroom.
Dad holding Billy out on a thick and bitten finger,
Saying *Here: Come on Joe—touch him.*
Every Sunday night the same.
Dad's quiet urging and
That laugh: *You've*
Got to be
Kidding,
Son.

CENTIPEDE

With the storm moved on the next town
we take a flashlight down to the basement

Nested chairs stripped of varnish
Turpentine shadows stiff legs in the air

Look by the fusebox a centipede Dad says
I scream and let go of his hairy arm

MY FATHER'S TELESCOPE

The oldest joke
in the world,
a chair on three legs.

Sawdust kicks
up, swirls
around his boots

and settles
in the cuffs of his
pants. The saw is

as nervous as
a parrot.
The chair

shrinks. After
years of cupboards
and end tables, after

a plywood Santa
and seven elves
for the lawn in snow,

he knows.
He's failed, and
in oak.

Next Christmas
he buys himself
and his son

a telescope.

SONG. SUMMER

Sexless, my brother flies
over the house. He is glad
to have this dark vegetable
taken from him and hums

as he circles. The air
brims; already forgotten
his name and the beckoning
shapes below on the lawn.

In the evening my brother
dips, a dark cross fluttering.
He hears the eaves
murmur; he watches the open

mouth of my father. Now
he smiles, sailing
over the roof, heading
straight for the blue cloud

of pine.

ANTI-FATHER

Contrary to
tales you told us

summer nights when
the air conditioner

broke—the stars
are not far

apart. Rather
they draw

closer together
with years.

And houses
shrivel, un-lost,

and porches sag;
neighbors phone

to report cracks
in the cellar floor,

roots of the willow
coming up. Stars

speak to a child.
The past

is silent. . . .
Just between

me and you,
woman to man,

outer space is
inconceivably

intimate.

TO BED

We turn off
the light and
walk upstairs.
Scurrile moon
and a crazed
sniper hugging
the roof, a nickel
and its buffalo.
The house is
strange, the screen
padlocked
for luck, for
riches, for
love, the cup
of water in my
hands dark
as a well.
Dark swells. The
last one up
is the first
to go.

A FATHER OUT WALKING
ON THE LAWN

Five rings light your approach across
the dark. You're lonely, anyone

can tell— so many of you
trembling, at the center the thick

dark root. Out here on a lawn
twenty-one years
gone under the haunches of a neighbor's

house, American Beauties
lining a driveway the mirror image of your own,

you wander, waiting to be
discovered. What
can I say to a body
that merely looks

like you? The willow, infatuated with its
surroundings, quakes; not that violent
orgasm nor the vain promise of

a rose relinquishing
its famous scent all for you, no,

not even the single
brilliant feather

a blue jay loses in flight
which dangles momentarily, azure scimitar,
above the warm eaves of your house—
nothing can change

this travesty, this
magician's skew of scarves
issuing from an opaque heart.

Who sees you anyway, except
at night, and with a fantastic eye?

If only you were bright enough to touch!

IV

PRIMER FOR THE NUCLEAR AGE

Doc, all my life people say
I was ugly. (pause) Makes me
feel mean.

—BORIS KARLOFF,
in *The Raven*

THE SAILOR IN AFRICA

a Viennese card game, circa 1910

There are two white captains
and two Moors. The pilots complement
their superiors, while the crew,
eight hands per master, wear
identical motley.
Available also, four ships
and a wild card
(starburst) which
luck can change into
a schooner or
a beautiful woman.

The captains, pilots, crews
commence
from the globe's four
corners. They share
a sun, a moon, and one
treasure. The goal
is Africa. One must uphold
the proportions between
superior and subordinate
while obtaining
chips. There are several cards
representing either
cannons or cannonballs
to make matters more
interesting. Plus a pair
of dice, for where
can we go without chance?

Say the Italian Moor
sails in sunshine
to Morocco and is rewarded
five black chips. Meanwhile
the British captain and
his swarthy pilot are stranded
with an overladen ship

somewhere between the Ibos and
Jamestown, Virginia.
The moon intrudes. When
the Spanish brigantine looms
on the horizon, they are actually
grateful, for they have cannons
and the Sevillian does not.

Both ships proceed
to Virginia. The arrow swings
east. Monsieur de la Roque
parades on deck, a small
white anchor stitched
on a blue field over
his heart. He surveys
his craft, finely strung
as a harp. *If all goes well
we'll reach Santo Domingo
tomorrow. . . .*

By now the Italian vessel
is safely through
the Suez Canal,
but a card shows "gale"
and it runs aground
on the western shore
of Madagascar, miraculously
unscathed. The captain falls
asleep on the beach, dreaming
of gold. Awake, he finds
ship and crew vanished, the
sun grinning and the treasure
secure at the bottom of the deck.
—Will he,

                    like the Spanish Moor,
be sold, merchant
to merchandise, or will
wild boars discover
him first? Monsieur de la Roque

has landed at Santo Domingo,
picking up rum and a slave
named Pedro. Such
flashing eyes and refined
manners! He'll make
an excellent valet.

Adrift in the Atlantic
again, the Englishman
plays quoits with his pilot,
his eyes raw
from staring into the sun.
A desperate man, he will
choose the beautiful woman
and die.

              While Pedro— who,
it turns out, is none other
than the Captain from Seville,
has loosened the leg irons
and drugged the fastidious
de la Roque! Now the
white anchor heaves
on the breast of the Moor, and
the sun beams on the mutinous
crew of his brother, who have
cleared the Cape of
Good Hope and are bearing
down on the Guinea coast.
Pedro heads

for Brazil— the women there,
he's heard, are prodigious!
Then the arrow swerves
due south, "gale" shows
from nowhere, the treasure
drops to the ocean floor.
At the sight of so many
mountains surging
whitely ahead, a crew hand,

thinking he has gone
to hell, falls
overboard, his red sash
flaring. Even

Pedro, lashed to the mast,
believes he has glimpsed
through the storm's
pearly membrane
God's dark face swooping
down to kiss— as the main
sail, incandescent under
pressure, bursts
like a star. The ship
splinters
on the rocks

        just as, deep
in the Madagascan forests,
a black hand
lifts from a nest
an egg the bright
green of malachite. . . .

At least one man happy
to have lost everything.
His crew will make it home
with tales of strange lands
and their captain's untimely
demise.

In the Atlantic,
windstill.
The English vessel, so
close to home, stalls.
Nothing for them to do
but pass the time
playing cards.

EARLY MORNING
ON THE TEL AVIV–HAIFA FREEWAY

The shore is cabbage green and reeks.
Reclaimed swamp sprouts citrus
and tamarisk, manna to the ancients
who were starved for miracles.
Now a paper mill and Alliance Tires
spill their secrets further out to sea.

Along the roadside, two Arab boys
drag a gull by the wings
and beyond a horse belly-up in the field.
A glider dips over us, silent, and
gleams as it turns. We should stop
but drive on.

WHY I TURNED VEGETARIAN

Mister Minister, I found
the tip of your thumb
bit off a way back:
a neat cap. Begging
your pardon, perhaps
you'd miss it
sooner or later.
You probably dropped it
folding the newspaper.

I don't mean to intrude.
I saw no other way less painful
or designed. It was lying
where I couldn't fail
to spot it—still fresh
with color and ridges
and a sliver of nail

and the teeth marks
showing—the only
edible mushroom
in the whole plot of grass.

EASTERN EUROPEAN ECLOGUES

I

This melodious
prison: crowds
shivering around
the sausage stalls.

II

One of us will
suffer. Don't move.
Not one word
more. You're
imagining things.

III

All that's quiet
is magic. Fields
steaming with dung.
Fresh meat in the air.

IV

One of us will need
a month in the country
to ward off imminent
complications.

V

Who?
Of course not.
Why should they.
Of course not.

VI

The countryside
is lovely
this time of year

FLIRTATION

After all, there's no need
to say anything

at first. An orange, peeled
and quartered, flares

like a tulip on a wedgwood plate.
Anything can happen.

Outside the sun
has rolled up her rugs

and night strewn salt
across the sky. My heart

is humming a tune
I haven't heard in years!

Quiet's cool flesh—
let's sniff and eat it.

There are ways
to make of the moment

a topiary
so the pleasure's in

walking through.

EXEUNT THE VIOLS

with their throb and yearn, their sad
stomach of an alley cat. Listen:

even the ocean mourns the passage
of voices so pure and penetrant, that

insect hum. Who discovered usefulness?
Who forgot how to sing, simply?

(Magnificence spoke up briefly, followed
by the race boat's break-neck

dazzle.) A tremor rises in the throat
of the cat, the quill jerks in the hand

of the melancholy scribe. The gambas
beat a retreat, gracefully—

their last chord a breath drawn
deep in a garden maze, there

near the statue
smiling under the stars.

THE LEFT-HANDED CELLIST

You came with a cello in one hand,
in the other, nothing.
Play, you said.

I played the scales of ignorant evenings.
I played in high heels to be closer to you.

When you snapped off a stem
from the vase, you broke
my little finger.

This is a theme in mauve:
it begins with the children's blind bodies,
it ends with the boys in the orchestra.

Tell me that you did not profit from me,
you with the pewter hands.

LINES MUTTERED IN SLEEP

Black chest hairs, soft sudden mass.
Washed up on her breast his pale and startled face.
Pine scent, lake scent, gorse scent, bark.

PRIMER FOR THE NUCLEAR AGE

At the edge of the mariner's
        map is written: "Beyond
        this point lie Monsters."

Someone left the light on
        in the pantry—there's
        a skull in there on the shelf

that talks. Blue eyes
        in the air, blue as
        an idiot's. Any fear, any

memory will do; and if you've
        got a heart at all, someday
        it will kill you.

PARSLEY

1. *The Cane Fields*

There is a parrot imitating spring
in the palace, its feathers parsley green.
Out of the swamp the cane appears

to haunt us, and we cut it down. El General
searches for a word; he is all the world
there is. Like a parrot imitating spring,

we lie down screaming as rain punches through
and we come up green. We cannot speak an R—
out of the swamp, the cane appears

and then the mountain we call in whispers *Katalina*.
The children gnaw their teeth to arrowheads.
There is a parrot imitating spring.

El General has found his word: *perejil.*
Who says it, lives. He laughs, teeth shining
out of the swamp. The cane appears

in our dreams, lashed by wind and streaming.
And we lie down. For every drop of blood
there is a parrot imitating spring.
Out of the swamp the cane appears.

2. The Palace

The word the general's chosen is parsley.
It is fall, when thoughts turn
to love and death; the general thinks
of his mother, how she died in the fall
and he planted her walking cane at the grave
and it flowered, each spring stolidly forming
four-star blossoms. The general

pulls on his boots, he stomps to
her room in the palace, the one without
curtains, the one with a parrot
in a brass ring. As he paces he wonders
Who can I kill today. And for a moment
the little knot of screams
is still. The parrot, who has traveled

all the way from Australia in an ivory
cage, is, coy as a widow, practising
spring. Ever since the morning
his mother collapsed in the kitchen
while baking skull-shaped candies
for the Day of the Dead, the general
has hated sweets. He orders pastries
brought up for the bird; they arrive

dusted with sugar on a bed of lace.
The knot in his throat starts to twitch;
he sees his boots the first day in battle
splashed with mud and urine
as a soldier falls at his feet amazed—
how stupid he looked!— at the sound
of artillery. *I never thought it would sing*
the soldier said, and died. Now

the general sees the fields of sugar
cane, lashed by rain and streaming.

He sees his mother's smile, the teeth
gnawed to arrowheads. He hears
the Haitians sing without R's
as they swing the great machetes:
Katalina, they sing, *Katalina*,

mi madle, mi amol en muelte. God knows
his mother was no stupid woman; she
could roll an R like a queen. Even
a parrot can roll an R! In the bare room
the bright feathers arch in a parody
of greenery, as the last pale crumbs
disappear under the blackened tongue. Someone

calls out his name in a voice
so like his mother's, a startled tear
splashes the tip of his right boot.
My mother, my love in death.
The general remembers the tiny green sprigs
men of his village wore in their capes
to honor the birth of a son. He will
order many, this time, to be killed

for a single, beautiful word.

THOMAS AND BEULAH

(1986)

*These poems tell two sides of a story
and are meant to be read in sequence.*

I

MANDOLIN

Black Boy, O Black Boy,
is the port worth the cruise?

—MELVIN B. TOLSON,
Harlem Gallery

THE EVENT

Ever since they'd left the Tennessee ridge
with nothing to boast of
but good looks and a mandolin,

the two Negroes leaning
on the rail of a riverboat
were inseparable: Lem plucked

to Thomas' silver falsetto.
But the night was hot and they were drunk.
They spat where the wheel

churned mud and moonlight,
they called to the tarantulas
down among the bananas

to come out and dance.
You're so fine and mighty; let's see
what you can do, said Thomas, pointing

to a tree-capped island.
Lem stripped, spoke easy: *Them's chestnuts,*
I believe. Dove

quick as a gasp. Thomas, dry
on deck, saw the green crown shake
as the island slipped

under, dissolved
in the thickening stream.
At his feet

a stinking circle of rags,
the half-shell mandolin.
Where the wheel turned the water

gently shirred.

VARIATION ON PAIN

Two strings, one pierced cry.
So many ways to imitate
The ringing in his ears.

He lay on the bunk, mandolin
In his arms. Two strings
For each note and seventeen
Frets; ridged sound
Humming beneath calloused
Fingertips.

There was a needle
In his head but nothing
Fit through it. Sound quivered
Like a rope stretched clear
To land, tensed and brimming,
A man gurgling air.

Two greased strings
For each pierced lobe:
So is the past forgiven.

JIVING

Heading North, straw hat
cocked on the back of his head,

tight curls gleaming
with brilliantine, he didn't stop

until the nights of chaw
and river-bright

had retreated, somehow
into another's life. He landed

in Akron, Ohio
1921,

on the dingy beach
of a man-made lake.

Since what he'd been through
he was always jiving, gold hoop

from the right ear jiggling
and a glass stud, bright blue

in his left. The young ladies
saying *He sure plays*

that tater bug
like the devil!

sighing their sighs
and dimpling.

STRAW HAT

In the city, under the saw-toothed leaves of an oak
overlooking the tracks, he sits out
the last minutes before dawn, lucky
to sleep third shift. Years before
he was anything, he lay on
so many kinds of grass, under stars,
the moon's bald eye opposing.

He used to sleep like a glass of water
held up in the hand of a very young girl.
Then he learned he wasn't perfect, that
no one was perfect. So he made his way
North under the bland roof of a tent
too small for even his lean body.

The mattress ticking he shares in the work barracks
is brown and smells
from the sweat of two other men.
One of them chews snuff:
he's never met either.
To him, work is a narrow grief
and the music afterwards
is like a woman
reaching into his chest
to spread it around. When he sings

he closes his eyes.
He **never** knows when she'll be coming
but **when** she leaves, he always
tips his hat.

COURTSHIP

1.

*Fine evening may I have
the pleasure . . .*
up and down the block
waiting—for what? A
magnolia breeze, someone
to trot out the stars?

But she won't set a foot
in his turtledove Nash,
it wasn't proper.
Her pleated skirt fans
softly, a circlet of arrows.

King of the Crawfish
in his yellow scarf,
mandolin belly pressed tight
to his hounds-tooth vest—

his wrist flicks for the pleats
all in a row, sighing . . .

2.

. . . so he wraps the yellow silk
still warm from his throat
around her shoulders. (He made
good money; he could buy another.)
A gnat flies
in his eye and she thinks
he's crying.

Then the parlor festooned
like a ship and Thomas
twirling his hat in his hands
wondering how did I get here.
China pugs guarding a fringed settee
where a father, half-Cherokee,
smokes and frowns.
I'll give her a good life—
what was he doing,
selling all for a song?
His heart fluttering shut
then slowly opening.

REFRAIN

The man inside the mandolin
plays a new tune
every night, sailing
past the bedroom window:

Take a gourd and string it
Take a banana and peel it
Buy a baby blue Nash
And wheel and deal it

Now he's raised a mast
and tied himself to it
with rags, drunker
than a robin on the wing:

Count your kisses
Sweet as honey
Count your boss'
Dirty money

The bed's oak
and clumsy, pitching
with its crew,
a man and a wife—

Now he's dancing, moving
only his feet. No way
to shut him up but
roll over, scattering

ruffles and silk,
stiff with a dog's breath
among lilies
and ripening skin:

Love on a raft
By the light o' the moon
And the bandit gaze
Of the old raccoon.

VARIATION ON GUILT

Count it anyway he wants—
by the waiting room clock,
by a lengthening hangnail,
by his buttons, the cigars crackling
in cellophane—

no explosion. No latch clangs
home. Perfect bystander, high
and dry with a scream caught
in his throat, he looks down

the row of faces coddled
in anxious pride. Wretched
little difference, he thinks,
between enduring pain and
waiting for pain
to work on others.

The doors fly apart—no,
he wouldn't run away!
It's a girl, he can tell
by that smirk, that strut of a mountebank!

But he doesn't feel a thing.
Weak with rage,
Thomas deals the cigars,
spits out the bitter tip in tears.

NOTHING DOWN

He lets her pick the color.
She saunters along the gleaming fenders
trying to guess his mind.

> *The flower*
> *dangled, blue flame*
> *above his head.*
> *He had stumbled into the woods*
> *and found this silent*
> *forgiveness.*

How they'd all talk!
Punkin and Babe,

Willemma tsk-tsking in her
sinking cabin,

a child's forest,
moss and threads
gone wild with hope

the boys down by the creek
grown now, straddling
the rail at the General Store . . .

Lem smiled from a tree
and nodded when Thomas told him
he was a few years early.
"We'll run away together,"
was all Lem said.

She bends over,
admiring her reflection
in the headlamp casing of a Peerless.

On an ordinary day
he would have plucked this
blue trumpet of Heaven
and rushed it home to water.

"Nigger Red,"
she drawls, moving on.

"Catching a woman," Lem used
to say, "is like rubbing
two pieces of silk together.
Done right, the sheen jags
and the grit shines through."

A sky blue Chandler!
She pauses, feeling his gaze.

Every male on the Ridge
old enough to whistle

was either in the woods
or under a porch.
He could hear the dogs
rippling up the hill.

Eight miles outside Murfreesboro
the burn of stripped rubber,
soft mud of a ditch.
A carload of white men
halloo past them on Route 231.
"You and your South!" she shouts
above the radiator hiss.
"Don't tell me this ain't what
you were hoping for."

The air was being torn
into hopeless pieces.
Only this flower hovering
above his head
couldn't hear the screaming.
That is why the petals had grown
so final.

THE ZEPPELIN FACTORY

The zeppelin factory
needed workers, all right—
but, standing in the cage
of the whale's belly, sparks
flying off the joints
and noise thundering,
Thomas wanted to sit
right down and cry.

That spring the third
largest airship was dubbed
the biggest joke
in town, though they all

turned out for the launch.
Wind caught,
"The Akron" floated
out of control,

three men in tow—
one dropped
to safety, one
hung on but the third,
muscles and adrenalin
failing, fell
clawing
six hundred feet.

Thomas at night
in the vacant lot:
 Here I am, intact
 and faint-hearted.

Thomas hiding
his heart with his hat
at the football game, eyeing
the Goodyear blimp overhead:
 Big boy I know
 you're in there.

UNDER THE VIADUCT, 1932

He avoided the empty millyards,
the households towering
next to the curb. It was dark
where he walked, although above him
the traffic was hissing.

He poked a trail in the mud
with his tin-capped stick.
If he had a son this time
he would teach him how to step

between his family and the police,
the mob bellowing
as a kettle of communal soup
spilled over a gray bank of clothes. . . .

The pavement wobbled, loosened by rain.
He liked it down here
where the luck of the mighty
had tumbled,

black suit and collarbone.
He could smell the worms stirring in their holes.
He could watch the white sheet settle
while all across the North Hill Viaduct

tires slithered to a halt.

LIGHTNIN' BLUES

On the radio a canary bewailed her luck
while the county outside was kicking with rain.
The kids bickered in the back seat;
the wife gasped whenever lightning struck
where it damn well pleased. Friday night,

and he never sang better. The fish
would be flashing like beautiful sequined cigars.
This time he'd fixed the bait himself,
cornmeal and a little sugar water
stirred to a ball on the stove,
pinched off for the scavenger carp.

So why did the car stall? And leap
backwards every time he turned the key?
Was Gabriel a paper man, a horn player
who could follow only the notes on the score?
Or was this sheriff the culprit,
pressing his badge to the window to say

You're lucky—a tree fell on the road ahead
just a few minutes ago.

Turned around, the car started
meek as a lamb. No one spoke
but that old trickster on the radio,
Kingfish addressing the Mystic Knights of the Sea.

COMPENDIUM

He gave up fine cordials and
his hounds-tooth vest.

He became a sweet tenor
in the gospel choir.

Canary, usurper
of his wife's affections.

Girl girl
girl girl.

In the parlor, with streamers,
a bug on a nail.

The canary courting its effigy.
The girls fragrant in their beds.

DEFINITION IN THE FACE OF UNNAMED FURY

That dragonfly, bloated, pinned
to the wall, its gossamer wings in tatters
(yellow silk, actually, faded in rivulets)—
what is it? A pendulum
with time on its hands, a frozen

teardrop, a winter melon
with a white, sweet flesh?

Go on—ask the canary.
Ask that sun-bleached delicacy
in its house of sticks
and it will answer *Pelican's bill.*
What else did you expect?

"How long has it been . . .?"
Too long. Each note slips
into querulous rebuke, fingerpads
scored with pain, shallow ditches
to rut in like a runaway slave
with a barking heart. Days afterwards
blisters to hide from the children.
Hanging by a thread. *Some day,*
he threatens, *I'll just
let go.*

AIRCRAFT

Too frail for combat, he stands
before an interrupted wing,
playing with an idea, nothing serious.
Afternoons, the hall gaped with aluminum
glaring, flying toward the sun; now
though, first thing in the morning, there is only
gray sheen and chatter
from the robust women around him
and the bolt waiting for his riveter's
five second blast.

The night before in the dark
of the peanut gallery, he listened to blouses shifting
and sniffed magnolias, white
tongues of remorse

sinking into the earth. Then
the newsreel leapt forward
into war.

Why *frail*? Why not simply
family man? Why wings, when
women with fingers no smaller than his
dabble in the gnarled intelligence of an engine?

And if he gave just a four second blast,
or three? Reflection is such

a bloodless light.
After lunch, they would bathe in fire.

AURORA BOREALIS

This far south such crippling
Radiance. People surge
From their homes onto the streets, certain
This is the end,
For it is 1943
And they are tired.

Thomas walks out of the movie house
And forgets where he is.
He is drowning and
The darkness above him
Spits and churns.

What shines is a thought
Which has lost its way. Helpless
It hangs and shivers
Like a veil. So much

For despair.
Thomas, go home.

VARIATION ON GAINING A SON

That shy angle of his daughter's head—
where did they all learn it?
And her soldier at tender attention,
waiting for the beloved to slide out
beneath the veil. Thomas knew

what he'd find there—a mocking smile, valiant
like that on the smooth face of the young sergeant
drilled neatly through the first minute of battle.
Women called it *offering up a kiss*.

He watched the bridegroom swallow.
For the first time Thomas felt like
calling him *Son*.

ONE VOLUME MISSING

Green sludge of a riverbank,
swirled and blotched,
as if a tree above him were shuffling
cards.
          Who would have thought
the binding of a "Standard Work
of Reference in the Arts,
Science, History, Discovery
and Invention" could bring back

slow afternoons with a line and bent nail

here, his wingtips balanced
on a scuffed linoleum square
at the basement rummage sale
of the A.M.E. Zion Church?

He opens *Motherwell-Orion* and finds
orchids on the frontispiece

overlain with tissue,
fever-specked and drooping
their inflamed penises.

Werner's Encyclopedia,
Akron, Ohio, 1909:
Complete in Twenty-Five Volumes
minus one—

for five bucks
no zebras, no Virginia,
no wars.

THE CHARM

They called us
the tater bug twins.
We could take a tune
and chew it up, fling
it to the moon
for the crows to eat.

At night he saw him,
naked and swollen
under the backyard tree.
No reason, he replied
when asked why he'd done
it. Thomas woke up
minutes later, thinking
What I need is a drink.

Sunday mornings
fried fish and hominy steaming
from the plates like an oracle.
The canary sang more furious
than ever, but he heard
the whisper: *I ain't dead.*
I just gave you my life.

GOSPEL

Swing low so I
can step inside—
a humming ship of voices
big with all

the wrongs done
done them.
No sound this generous
could fail:

ride joy until
it cracks like an egg,
make sorrow
seethe and whisper.

From a fortress
of animal misery
soars the chill voice
of the tenor, enraptured

with sacrifice.
What do I see,
he complains, notes
brightly rising

towards a sky
blank with promise.
Yet how healthy
the single contralto

settling deeper
into her watery furs!
Carry me home,
she cajoles, bearing

down. Candelabras
brim. But he slips
through God's net and swims
heavenward, warbling.

ROAST POSSUM

The possum's a greasy critter
that lives on persimmons and what
the Bible calls carrion.
So much from the 1909 Werner
Encyclopedia, three rows of deep green
along the wall. A granddaughter
propped on each knee,
Thomas went on with his tale—

but it was for Malcolm, little
Red Delicious, that he invented
embellishments: *We shined that possum*
with a torch and I shinnied up,
being the smallest,
to shake him down. He glared at me,
teeth bared like a shark's
in that torpedo snout.
Man he was tough but no match
for old-time know-how.

Malcolm hung back, studying them
with his gold hawk eyes. When the girls
got restless, Thomas talked horses:
Strolling Jim, who could balance
a glass of water on his back
and trot the village square
without spilling a drop. Who put
Wartrace on the map and was buried
under a stone, like a man.

They liked that part.
He could have gone on to tell them
that the Werner admitted Negro children
to be intelligent, though briskness
clouded over at puberty, bringing
indirection and laziness. Instead,
he added: *You got to be careful*
with a possum when he's on the ground;

he'll turn on his back and play dead
till you give up looking. That's
what you'd call sullin'.

Malcolm interrupted to ask
who owned Strolling Jim,
and who paid for the tombstone.
They stared each other down
man to man, before Thomas,
as a grandfather, replied:
                              Yessir,
we enjoyed that possum. We ate him
real slow, with sweet potatoes.

THE STROKE

Later he'll say Death stepped right up
to shake his hand, then squeezed
until he sank to his knees. *(Get up,*
nigger. Get up and try again.)

Much later he'll admit he'd been afraid,
curled tight in the center of the rug, sunlight
striking one cheek and plaited raffia
scratching the other. He'll leave out

the part about daydream's aromatic fields
and the strap-worn flanks of the mule
he followed through them. When his wife asks
how did it feel, he won't mention

that the sun shone like the summer
she was pregnant with their first, and
that she craved watermelon which he smuggled
home wrapped in a newspaper, and how

the bus driver smirked as his nickel
clicked through—no, he'll say

it was like being kicked by a mule.
Right now, though, pinned to the bull's-eye,

he knows it was Lem all along:
Lem's knuckles tapping his chest in passing,
Lem's heart, for safekeeping,
he shores up in his arms.

THE SATISFACTION COAL COMPANY

1.

What to do with a day.
Leaf through *Jet*. Watch T.V.
Freezing on the porch
but he goes anyhow, snow too high
for a walk, the ice treacherous.
Inside, the gas heater takes care of itself;
he doesn't even notice being warm.

Everyone says he looks great.
Across the street a drunk stands smiling
at something carved in a tree.
The new neighbor with the floating hips
scoots out to get the mail
and waves once, brightly,
storm door clipping her heel on the way in.

2.

Twice a week he had taken the bus down Glendale Hill
to the corner of Market. Slipped through
the alley by the canal and let himself in.
Started to sweep
with terrible care, like a woman
brushing shine into her hair,
same motion, same lullaby.

No curtains—the cop on the beat
stopped outside once in the hour
to swing his billy club and glare.

It was better on Saturdays
when the children came along:
he mopped while they emptied
ashtrays, clang of glass on metal
then a dry scutter. Next they counted
nailheads studding the leather cushions.
Thirty-four! they shouted,
that was the year and
they found it mighty amusing.

But during the week he noticed more—
lights when they gushed or dimmed
at the Portage Hotel, the 10:32
picking up speed past the B & O switchyard,
floorboards trembling and the explosive
kachook kachook kachook kachook
and the oiled rails ticking underneath.

3.

They were poor then but everyone had been poor.
He hadn't minded the sweeping,
just the thought of it—like now
when people ask him what he's thinking
and he says *I'm listening.*

Those nights walking home alone,
the bucket of coal scraps banging his knee,
he'd hear a roaring furnace
with its dry, familiar heat. Now the nights
take care of themselves—as for the days,
there is the canary's sweet curdled song,
the wino smiling through his dribble.
Past the hill, past the gorge
choked with wild sumac in summer,

the corner has been upgraded.
Still, he'd like to go down there someday
to stand for a while, and get warm.

THOMAS AT THE WHEEL

This, then, the river he had to swim.
Through the wipers the drugstore
shouted, lit up like a casino,
neon script leering from the shuddering asphalt.

Then the glass doors flew apart
and a man walked out to the curb
to light a cigarette. Thomas thought
the sky was emptying itself as fast
as his chest was filling with water.

Should he honk? What a joke—
he couldn't ungrip the steering wheel.
The man looked him calmly in the eye
and tossed the match away.

And now the street dark, not a soul
nor its brother. He lay down across
the seat, a pod set to sea,
a kiss unpuckering. He watched
the slit eye of the glove compartment,
the prescription inside,

he laughed as he thought *Oh
the writing on the water.* Thomas imagined
his wife as she awoke missing him,
cracking a window. He heard sirens
rise as the keys swung, ticking.

II

CANARY IN BLOOM

Ah, how the senses flood at my repeating,
As once in her fire-lit heart I felt the furies
Beating, beating.

—ANNE SPENCER,
"Lines to a Nasturtium"

TAKING IN WASH

Papa called her Pearl when he came home
drunk, swaying as if the wind touched
only him. Towards winter his skin paled,
buckeye to ginger root, cold drawing
the yellow out. The Cherokee in him,
Mama said. Mama never changed:
when the dog crawled under the stove
and the back gate slammed, Mama hid
the laundry. Sheba barked as she barked
in snow or clover, a spoiled and ornery bitch.

She was Papa's girl,
black though she was. Once,
in winter, she walked through a dream
all the way down the stairs
to stop at the mirror, a beast
with stricken eyes
who screamed the house awake. Tonight

every light hums, the kitchen arctic
with sheets. Papa is making the hankies
sail. Her foot upon a silk
stitched rose, she waits
until he turns, his smile sliding all over.
Mama a tight dark fist.
Touch that child

and I'll cut you down
just like the cedar of Lebanon.

MAGIC

Practice makes perfect, the old folks said.
So she rehearsed deception
until ice cubes
dangled willingly

from a plain white string
and she could change
an egg into her last nickel.
Sent to the yard to sharpen,

she bent so long over
the wheel the knives
grew thin. When she stood up,
her brow shorn clean
as a wheatfield and
stippled with blood,
she felt nothing, even
when Mama screamed.

She fed sauerkraut to the apple tree;
the apples bloomed tarter
every year. Like all art
useless and beautiful, like
sailing in air,

things happened
to her. One night she awoke
and on the lawn blazed
a scaffolding strung in lights.
Next morning the Sunday paper
showed the Eiffel Tower
soaring through clouds.
It was a sign

she would make it to Paris one day.

COURTSHIP, DILIGENCE

A yellow scarf runs through his fingers
as if it were melting.
Thomas dabbing his brow.

And now his mandolin in a hurry
though the night, as they say,
is young,
though she is *getting on*.

Hush, the strings tinkle. *Pretty gal.*

Cigar-box music!
She'd much prefer a pianola
and scent in a sky-colored flask.

Not that scarf, bright as butter.
Not his hands, cool as dimes.

PROMISES

*Each hurt swallowed
is a stone.* Last words
whispered to his daughter
as he placed her fingertips
lightly into the palm
of her groom.

She smiled upwards
to Jesus, then Thomas,
turning her back as
politely as possible.
If that were the case
he was a mountain of shame.

Poised on the stone
steps of the church,
she tried to forget
his hulk in the vestibule,
clumsy in blue serge,
his fingers worrying the
lucky bead in his pocket.

Beneath the airborne bouquet
was a meadow of virgins
urging *Be water, be light.*
A deep breath, and she plunged
through sunbeams and kisses,
rice drumming
the both of them blind.

DUSTING

Every day a wilderness—no
shade in sight. Beulah
patient among knicknacks,
the solarium a rage
of light, a grainstorm
as her gray cloth brings
dark wood to life.

Under her hand scrolls
and crests gleam
darker still. What
was his name, that
silly boy at the fair with
the rifle booth? And his kiss and
the clear bowl with one bright
fish, rippling
wound!

Not Michael—
something finer. Each dust
stroke a deep breath and
the canary in bloom.
Wavery memory: home
from a dance, the front door
blown open and the parlor
in snow, she rushed
the bowl to the stove, watched
as the locket of ice

dissolved and he
swam free.

That was years before
Father gave her up
with her name, years before
her name grew to mean
Promise, then
Desert-in-Peace.
Long before the shadow and
sun's accomplice, the tree.

Maurice.

A HILL OF BEANS

One spring the circus gave
free passes and there was music,
the screens unlatched
to let in starlight. At the well,
a monkey tipped her his fine red hat
and drank from a china cup.
By mid-morning her cobblers
were cooling on the sill.
Then the tents folded and the grass

grew back with a path
torn waist-high to the railroad
where the hoboes jumped the slow curve
just outside Union Station.
She fed them while they talked,
easy in their rags. *Any two points
make a line*, they'd say,
and we're gonna ride them all.

Cat hairs
came up with the dipper;
Thomas tossed on his pillow

as if at sea. When money failed
for peaches, she pulled
rhubarb at the edge of the field.
Then another man showed up
in her kitchen and she smelled
fear in his grimy overalls,
the pale eyes bright as salt.

There wasn't even pork
for the navy beans. But he ate
straight down to the blue
bottom of the pot and rested
there a moment, hardly breathing.
That night she made Thomas
board up the well.
Beyond the tracks, the city blazed
as if looks were everything.

WEATHERING OUT

She liked mornings the best—Thomas gone
to look for work, her coffee flushed with milk,

outside autumn trees blowsy and dripping.
Past the seventh month she couldn't see her feet

so she floated from room to room, houseshoes flapping,
navigating corners in wonder. When she leaned

against a door jamb to yawn, she disappeared entirely.

Last week they had taken a bus at dawn
to the new airdock. The hangar slid open in segments

and the zeppelin nosed forward in its silver envelope.
The men walked it out gingerly, like a poodle,

then tied it to a mast and went back inside.
Beulah felt just that large and placid, a lake;

she glistened from cocoa butter smoothed in
when Thomas returned every evening nearly

in tears. He'd lean an ear on her belly
and say: *Little fellow's really talking,*

though to her it was more the *pok-pok-pok*
of a fingernail tapping a thick cream lampshade.

Sometimes during the night she woke and found him
asleep there and the child sleeping, too.

The coffee was good but too little. Outside
everything shivered in tinfoil—only the clover

between the cobblestones hung stubbornly on,
green as an afterthought. . . .

MOTHERHOOD

She dreams the baby's so small she keeps
misplacing it—it rolls from the hutch
and the mouse carries it home, it disappears
with his shirt in the wash.
Then she drops it and it explodes
like a watermelon, eyes spitting.

Finally they get to the countryside;
Thomas has it in a sling.
He's strewing rice along the road
while the trees chitter with tiny birds.
In the meadow to their right three men
are playing rough with a white wolf. She calls

warning but the wolf breaks free
and she runs, the rattle
rolls into the gully, then she's
there and tossing the baby behind her,
listening for its cry as she straddles
the wolf and circles its throat, counting
until her thumbs push through to the earth.
White fur seeps red. She is hardly breathing.
The small wild eyes
go opaque with confusion and shame, like a child's.

ANNIVERSARY

Twelve years to the day
he puts the blue worry bead into his mouth.
The trick is to swallow your good luck, too.
Last words to a daughter . . .
and a wink to remember him by.

THE HOUSE ON BISHOP STREET

No front yard to speak of,
just a porch cantilevered on faith
where she arranged the canary's cage.
The house stayed dark all year
though there was instant light and water.
(No more gas jets hissing,

their flicker glinting off
Anna Rettich's midwife spectacles
as she whispered *think a baby*
and the babies came.) Spring
brought a whiff of cherries, the kind
you boiled for hours in sugar and cloves

from the yard of the Jewish family next door.
Yumanski refused to speak so
she never bought his vegetables
at the Canal Street Market. Gertrude,
his youngest and blondest,
slipped by mornings for bacon and grits.
There were summer floods and mildew

humming through fringe, there was
a picture of a ship she passed
on her way to the porch, strangers calling
from the street *Ma'am, your bird
shore can sing!* If she leaned out she could glimpse
the faintest of mauve—no more than an idea—
growing just behind the last houses.

DAYSTAR

She wanted a little room for thinking:
but she saw diapers steaming on the line,
a doll slumped behind the door.

So she lugged a chair behind the garage
to sit out the children's naps.

Sometimes there were things to watch—
the pinched armor of a vanished cricket,
a floating maple leaf. Other days
she stared until she was assured
when she closed her eyes
she'd see only her own vivid blood.

She had an hour, at best, before Liza appeared
pouting from the top of the stairs.
And just *what* was mother doing
out back with the field mice? Why,

building a palace. Later
that night when Thomas rolled over and
lurched into her, she would open her eyes
and think of the place that was hers
for an hour—where
she was nothing,
pure nothing, in the middle of the day.

OBEDIENCE

That smokestack, for instance,
in the vacant lot across the street:
if she could order it down and watch
it float in lapse-time over buckled tar and macadam
it would stop an inch or two perhaps
before her patent leather shoes.

Her body's no longer tender, but her mind is free.
She can think up a twilight, sulfur
flicking orange then black
as the tip of a flamingo's wing, the white
picket fence marching up the hill . . .

but she would never create such puny stars.
The house, shut up like a pocket watch,
those tight hearts breathing inside—
she could never invent them.

THE GREAT PALACES OF VERSAILLES

Nothing nastier than a white person!
She mutters as she irons alterations
in the backroom of Charlotte's Dress Shoppe.
The steam rising from a cranberry wool
comes alive with perspiration

and stale Evening of Paris.
Swamp she born from, swamp
she swallow, swamp she got to sink again.

The iron shoves gently
into a gusset, waits until
the puckers bloom away. Beyond
the curtain, the white girls are all
wearing shoulder pads to make their faces
delicate. That laugh would be Autumn,
tossing her hair in imitation of Bacall.

Beulah had read in the library
how French ladies at court would tuck
their fans in a sleeve
and walk in the gardens for air. Swaying
among lilies, lifting shy layers of silk,
they dropped excrement as daintily
as handkerchieves. Against all rules

she had saved the lining from a botched coat
to face last year's gray skirt. She knows
whenever she lifts a knee
she flashes crimson. That seems legitimate;
but in the book she had read
how the *cavaliere* amused themselves
wearing powder and perfume and spraying
yellow borders knee-high on the stucco
of the *Orangerie.*

A hanger clatters
in the front of the shoppe.
Beulah remembers how
even Autumn could lean into a settee
with her ankles crossed, sighing
I need a man who'll protect me
while smoking her cigarette down to the very end.

POMADE

She sweeps the kitchen floor of the river bed her husband saw fit
to bring home with his catfish, recalling
a flower—very straight,
with a spiked collar arching
under a crown of bright fluffy worms—
she had gathered in armfuls
along a still road in Tennessee. Even then
he was forever off in the woods somewhere in search
of a magic creek.

It **was** Willemma shushed the pack of dusty children
and **took** her inside the leaning cabin with its little
window in the door, the cutout magazine cloud taped to the pane
so's I'll always have shade. It was Willemma
showed her how to rub the petals fine
and heat them slow in mineral oil
until the skillet exhaled pears and nuts and rotting fir.

That cabin leaned straight away
to the south, took the very slant of heaven
through the crabgrass and Queen Anne's Lace to
the Colored Cemetery down in Wartrace. Barley soup
yearned toward the bowl's edge, the cornbread
hot from the oven climbed in glory
to the very black lip of the cast iron pan . . .
but Willemma stood straight as the day
she walked five miles to town for Scotch tape
and back again. Gaslight flickered on the cockeyed surface
of rain water in a galvanized pail in the corner
while Thomas pleaded with his sister
to get out while she still was fit.

Beebalm. The fragrance always put her
in mind of Turkish minarets against
a sky wrenched blue,
sweet and merciless. Willemma could wear her gray hair twisted
in two knots at the temples and still smell like travel.
But all those years she didn't budge. She simply turned

one day from slicing a turnip into a pot
when her chest opened and the inrushing air
knocked her down. *Call the reverend, I'm in the floor*
she called out to a passerby.

Beulah gazes through the pale speckled linoleum
to the webbed loam with its salt and worms. She smooths
her hair, then sniffs her palms. On the countertop
the catfish grins
like an oriental gentleman. Nothing ever stops. She feels
herself slowly rolling down the sides of the earth.

HEADDRESS

The hat on the table
in the dining room
is no pet trained
to sit still. Three
pearl-tipped spears and Beulah
maneuvering her shadow
to the floor. The hat
is cold. The hat
wants more.

(The customer will be
generous when satisfied
beyond belief. Spangled
tulle, then, in green
and gold and sherry.)

Beulah
would have settled
for less. She doesn't
pray when she's
terrified, sometimes, in-
side her skin like
today, humming
through a mouthful of pins.

Finished it's a mountain
on a dish, a capitol
poised on a littered shore.
The brim believes
in itself, its
double rose and feathers
ashiver. Extravagance
redeems. O
intimate parasol
that teaches to walk
with grace along beauty's seam.

SUNDAY GREENS

She wants to hear
wine pouring.
She wants to taste
change. She wants
pride to roar through
the kitchen till it shines
like straw, she wants

lean to replace
tradition. Ham knocks
in the pot, nothing
but bones, each
with its bracelet
of flesh.

The house stinks
like a zoo in summer,
while upstairs
her man sleeps on.
Robe slung over
her arm and
the cradled hymnal,

she pauses, remembers
her mother in a slip
lost in blues,
and those collards,
wild-eared,
singing.

RECOVERY

He's tucked his feet into corduroy scuffs
and gone out to the porch. From the parlor
with its glassed butterflies, the mandolin on the wall,
she can see one bare heel bobbing.

Years ago he had promised to take her to Chicago.
He was lovely then, a pigeon
whose pulse could be seen when the moment
was perfectly still. In the house

the dark rises and whirrs like a loom.
She stands by the davenport,
obedient among her trinkets,
secrets like birdsong in the air.

NIGHTMARE

She's dreaming
of salt again:
salt stinging her eyes,
making pepper of her hair,
salt in her panties
and the light all over.
If she wakes
she'll find him
gone and the dog
barking its tail off,

locked outside in the
dead of night.

Lids pinched shut,
she forces the itching
away. That streetlamp
through the window:
iridescent grit. As a girl
she once opened
an umbrella in the house
and her mother cried
you'll ruin us!
but that was so
long ago. Then
she wakes up.

WINGFOOT LAKE

(Independence Day, 1964)

On her 36th birthday, Thomas had shown her
her first swimming pool. It had been
his favorite color, exactly—just
so much of it, the swimmers' white arms jutting
into the chevrons of high society.
She had rolled up her window
and told him to drive on, fast.

Now this *act of mercy*: four daughters
dragging her to their husbands' company picnic,
white families on one side and them
on the other, unpacking the same
squeeze bottles of Heinz, the same
waxy beef patties and Salem potato chip bags.
So he was dead for the first time
on Fourth of July—ten years ago

had been harder, waiting for something to happen,
and ten years before that, the girls

like young horses eyeing the track.
Last August she stood alone for hours
in front of the T.V. set
as a crow's wing moved slowly through
the white streets of government.
That brave swimming

scared her, like Joanna saying
Mother, we're Afro-Americans now!
What did she know about Africa?
Were there lakes like this one
with a rowboat pushed under the pier?
Or Thomas' Great Mississippi
with its sullen silks? (There was
the Nile but the Nile belonged

to God.) Where she came from
was the past, 12 miles into town
where nobody had locked their back door,
and Goodyear hadn't begun to dream of a park
under the company symbol, a white foot
sprouting two small wings.

COMPANY

No one can help him anymore.
Not the young thing next door
in the red pedal pushers,
not the canary he drove distracted

with his mandolin. There'll be
no more trees to wake him in moonlight,
nor a single dry spring morning
when the fish are lonely for company.

She's standing there telling him: give it up.
She is weary of sirens and his face
worn with salt. *If this is code,*

she tells him, *listen: we were good,*
though we never believed it.
And now he can't even touch her feet.

THE ORIENTAL BALLERINA

twirls on the tips of a carnation
while the radio scratches out a morning hymn.
Daylight has not ventured as far

as the windows—the walls are still dark,
shadowed with the ghosts
of oversized gardenias. The ballerina

pirouettes to the wheeze of the old
rugged cross, she lifts
her shoulders past the edge

of the jewelbox lid. Two pink slippers
touch the ragged petals, no one
should have feet that small! In China

they do everything upside down:
this ballerina has not risen but drilled
a tunnel straight to America

where the bedrooms of the poor
are papered in vulgar flowers
on a background the color of grease, of

teabags, of cracked imitation walnut veneer.
On the other side of the world
they are shedding robes sprigged with

roses, roses drifting with a hiss
to the floor by the bed
as, here, the sun finally strikes the windows

suddenly opaque,
noncommital as shields. In this room
is a bed where the sun has gone

walking. Where a straw nods over
the lip of its glass and a hand
reaches for a tissue, crumpling it to a flower.

The ballerina has been drilling all night!
She flaunts her skirts like sails,
whirling in a disk so bright,

so rapidly she is standing still.
The sun walks the bed to the pillow
and pauses for breath (in the Orient,

breath floats like mist
in the fields), hesitating
at a knotted handkerchief that has slid

on its string and has lodged beneath
the right ear which discerns
the most fragile music

where there is none. The ballerina dances
at the end of a tunnel of light,
she spins on her impossible toes—

the rest is shadow.
The head on the pillow sees nothing
else, though it feels the sun warming

its cheeks. *There is no China;*
no cross, just the papery kiss
of a Kleenex above the stink of camphor,

the walls exploding with shabby tutus. . . .

CHRONOLOGY

1900:   Thomas born in Wartrace, Tennessee.

1904:   Beulah born in Rockmart, Georgia.

1906:   Beulah's family moves to Akron.

1916:   30,000 workers migrate to Akron.

1919:   Thomas leaves Tennessee for the riverboat life.

1921:   Thomas arrives in Akron.

1922:   Completion of viaduct spanning the Little Cuyahoga River.

1924:   December wedding.

1926:   First child born (Rose).

1928:   New car bought for the trip to Tennessee.

1929:   The Goodyear Zeppelin Airdock is built—the largest building in the world without interior supports.

1930:   Lose car due to the Depression. Second child born (Agnes).

1931:   The airship *Akron* disaster.

1932:   Vice-President of First Central Trust Company commits suicide. A union organizer is killed trying to aid an evicted family.

1932:   November: Third child born (Liza).

1934:   Part-time work cleaning offices of the Satisfaction Coal Company.

1935:   Fourth child born (Joanna). They move to Bishop Street.

1940:   11,000 Negroes living in Akron (total population: 243,000).

1942:   Thomas employed at Goodyear Aircraft in war relief work.

1945:   Rose marries a war veteran.

1946:   Thomas quits the gospel choir at the A.M.E. Zion Church.

1946:   Beulah takes a part-time job in Charlotte's Dress Shoppe.

1947:   First grandchild (Pauline) born to Rose.

1949:   Second grandchild (Jacqueline) born to Rose.

1950:   Beulah takes up millinery.

1951:   The only grandson (Malcolm) born to Agnes.

1956:   All daughters have been married off.

1960:   Thomas has first heart attack.

1963:   End of July: Thomas dies.

1963:   August: The March on Washington.

1964:   Beulah's daughters invite her to a Fourth of July picnic.

1966:   Beulah afflicted with glaucoma. She takes to her bed.

1969:   April: Beulah dies.

GRACE NOTES

(1989)

SUMMIT BEACH, 1921

The Negro beach jumped to the twitch
of an oil drum tattoo and a mandolin,
sweaters flying off the finest brown shoulders
this side of the world.

She sat by the fire, shawl moored
by a single fake cameo. She was cold,
thank you, she did not care to dance—
the scar on her knee winking
with the evening chill.

Papa had said don't be so fast,
you're all you've got. So she refused
to cut the wing, though she let the boys
bring her sassafras tea and drank it down
neat as a dropped hankie.

Her knee had itched in the cast
till she grew mean from bravery.
She could wait, she was gold.
When the right man smiled it would be
music skittering up her calf

like a chuckle. She could feel
the breeze in her ears like water,
like the air as a child when
she climbed Papa's shed and stepped off
the tin roof into blue,

with her parasol and invisible wings.

I

All water has a perfect memory and is forever
trying to get back to where it was.

—TONI MORRISON

SILOS

Like martial swans in spring paraded against the city sky's
shabby blue, they were always too white and
suddenly there.

They were never fingers, never xylophones, although once
a stranger said they put him in mind of Pan's pipes
and all the lost songs of Greece. But to the townspeople
they were like cigarettes, the smell chewy and bitter
like a field shorn of milkweed, or beer brewing, or
a fingernail scorched over a flame.

No, no, exclaimed the children. They're a fresh packet of chalk,
dreading math work.

They were masculine toys. They were tall wishes. They
were the ribs of the modern world.

FIFTH GRADE AUTOBIOGRAPHY

I was four in this photograph fishing
with my grandparents at a lake in Michigan.
My brother squats in poison ivy.
His Davy Crockett cap
sits squared on his head so the raccoon tail
flounces down the back of his sailor suit.

My grandfather sits to the far right
in a folding chair,
and I know his left hand is on
the tobacco in his pants pocket
because I used to wrap it for him
every Christmas. Grandmother's hips
bulge from the brush, she's leaning
into the ice chest, sun through the trees
printing her dress with soft
luminous paws.

I am staring jealously at my brother;
the day before he rode his first horse, alone.
I was strapped in a basket
behind my grandfather.
He smelled of lemons. He's died—

but I remember his hands.

THE BUCKEYE

We learned about the state tree
in school—its fruit
so useless, so ugly

no one bothered to
commend the smudged trunk
nor the slim leaves shifting

over our heads. Yet
they were a good thing to kick
along gutters

on the way home,
though they stank like
a drunk's piss in the roads

where cars had smashed
them. And in autumn
when the spiny helmets split

open,
there was the bald
seed with its wheat-

colored eye.
We loved
the modest countenance beneath

that leathery cap.
We, too, did not want to leave
our mothers.

We piled them up
for ammunition.
We lay down

with them
among the bruised leaves
so that we could

rise, shining.

QUAKER OATS

The grain elevators have stood empty for years. They used to feed an entire nation of children. Hunched in red leatherette breakfast-nooks, fingers dreaming, children let their spoons clack on the white sides of their bowls. They stare at the carton on the table, a miniature silo with a kindly face smiling under a stiff black hat.

They eat their oats with milk and butter and sugar. They eat their oats in their sleep, where horsedrawn carts jolt along miry roads, past cabins where other children wait, half-frozen under tattered counterpanes. The man with the black hat, a burlap sack tucked under his arm, steps down from the wagon whispering *come out, don't be afraid.*

And they come, the sick and the healthy; the red, the brown, the white; the ruddy and the sallow; the curly and the lank. They tumble from rafters and crawl out of trundles. He gives them to eat. He gives them prayers and a good start in the morning. He gives them free enterprise; he gives them the flag and PA systems and roller skates and citizenship. He gives them a tawny canoe to portage overland, through the woods, through the midwestern snow.

FLASH CARDS

In math I was the whiz kid, keeper
of oranges and apples. *What you don't understand,
master*, my father said; the faster
I answered, the faster they came.

I could see one bud on the teacher's geranium,
one clear bee sputtering at the wet pane.
The tulip trees always dragged after heavy rain
so I tucked my head as my boots slapped home.

My father put up his feet after work
and relaxed with a highball and *The Life of Lincoln*.
After supper we drilled and I climbed the dark

before sleep, before a thin voice hissed
numbers as I spun on a wheel. I had to guess.
Ten, I kept saying, *I'm only ten*.

CRAB-BOIL

(Ft. Myers, 1962)

Why do I remember the sky
above the forbidden beach,
why only blue and the scratch,
shell on tin, of their distress?
The rest

imagination supplies:
bucket and angry pink beseeching
claws. Why does Aunt Helen
laugh before saying "Look at that—

a bunch of niggers, not
a-one get out 'fore the others pull him
back." I don't believe her—

just as I don't believe *they* won't come
and chase us back to the colored-only shore
crisp with litter and broken glass.

"When do we kill them?"
"Kill 'em? Hell, the water does *that*.
They don't feel a thing . . . no nervous system."

I decide to believe this: I'm hungry.
Dismantled, they're merely exotic,
a blushing meat. After all, she *has*
grown old in the South. If
we're kicked out now, I'm ready.

HULLY GULLY

Locked in bathrooms for hours,
daydreaming in kitchens
as they leaned their elbows
into the shells of lemons,

they were humming, they were humming
Hully Gully. Summer lasted

a long time; porch geraniums
rocked the grandmothers to sleep
as night slugged in, moon riding the sky
like a drop of oil on water. Then down
the swollen pitch of avenue
discourteous blouses, bright rifflings,
gum popping to an invisible beat,

daughters floating above the ranks of bobby socks.
Theirs was a field to lie down in
while fathers worked swing shift and
wives straightened oval photographs
above the exhausted chenille
in bedrooms upstairs everywhere. . . .

FANTASY AND SCIENCE FICTION

On my knees in the dark I looked out
the front door of my parents' house
and across the street saw an identical
stoop, the porthole glass
wreathed in pine boughs with a flat red bow.
I knew if I crossed the street and entered,
taking living room, stairwell and landing
in reverse, I'd end up on my knees
in a house my parents never owned nor dreamed of owning
in the dark not daring
to open my eyes.

꒰

The skyscraper was happy
alone, willow-like
on the edge of the frontier,
nestled in oak and Iroquois.
Its elevators whooshed and chimed
and the sky ionized indigo, readied
for storm. Moccasins inched closer
while far away in a field,
Ben and his silver key make history
and the skyscraper, suddenly aware
of its goofy reverie,
is swallowed into mud like a godhead.

꒰

Give the village idiot back
his rose, why tease a stupid boy?
So what if it's a full-blown green?
Children are always imagining things.
Sometimes, shutting a book and rising,
you can walk off the back porch
and into the sea—though
it's not the sort of story
you'd tell your mother.

SISTERS

for Robin Dove Waynesboro

This is the one we called
Bird of the Dead, Double Bird
Who Feeds on Carrion. Dark
with a red organdy dress
for her third birthday,
she cried and cried,
snap-eyed imp whose brow sprouted horns
whenever she screwed up her face.

"Buzzard!" we shrieked
and when that was forbidden:
"Schmawk Schmawk Bird!" after the local radio
personality. Several beatings later
the first literary effort appeared, a story
called "Blank the Buzzard,"
for which I claimed the First Amendment.
It was confiscated and shredded.

I can't believe she's taller
than me now, that my smile
lines sag where her Indian cheekbones soar.
This is my home, my knothole
we're posing in front of. The palm tree
throws a boa across our shoulders.
Light seals the cracks.

UNCLE MILLET

He'd slip a rubber band around a glass of rye,
pluck it with one pearly nail
like a song he couldn't get off his mind.

Twice-widowed, down from Toronto to cool his heels,
he kept up the tales of nylons
stuffed hastily into coat pockets,

an aproned great-aunt settling
her bulk onto the front porch swing
just as Baby Sister vaulted the backyard gate. . . .

Sure, he was no good. And I wasn't
allowed over when he pulled into town.
But I memorized the stories, imagining
Canada full of men who'd use
a knife to defend their right to say:

Man, she was butter
just waiting to melt.

POEM IN WHICH I
REFUSE CONTEMPLATION

A letter from my mother was waiting:
read in standing, one a.m.,
just arrived at my German mother-in-law's

six hours from Paris by car.
Our daughter hops on Oma's bed,
happy to be back in a language

she knows. *Hello, all! Your postcard*
came on the nineth—familiar misspelled
words, exclamations. I wish my body

wouldn't cramp and leak; I want to—
as my daughter says, pretending to be
"Papa"—pull on boots and go for a long walk

alone. *Your cousin Ronnie in D.C.—*
remember him?—he was the one
a few months younger than you—

was strangulated at some chili joint,
your Aunt May is beside herself!
Mom skips to the garden which is

producing—onions, swiss chard,
lettuce, lettuce, lettuce, turnip greens and more lettuce
so far! The roses are flurishing.

Haven't I always hated gardening? And German,
with its patient, grunting building blocks,
and for that matter, English, too,

Americanese's chewy twang? *Raccoons*
have taken up residence
we were ten *in the crawl space*

but I can't feel his hand *who knows*
anymore *how we'll get them out?*
I'm still standing. Bags to unpack.

That's all for now. Take care.

II

The legendary forbidden fruit is the self.

—DAVID MCFADDEN

To inhabit was the most natural joy when I was still living inside; all was garden and I had not lost the way in.

—HÉLÈNE CIXOUS

MISSISSIPPI

In the beginning was the dark
moan and creak, a sidewheel
moving through. Thicker
then, scent of lilac,
scent of thyme; slight hairs
on a wrist lying down in sweat.
We were falling down
river, carnal
slippage and shadow melt.
We were standing on the deck
of the New World, before maps:
tepid seizure of a breeze
and the spirit hissing away . . .

AFTER STORM

Already the desert sky had packed
its scarves and gone over the hard blue hills
when I awoke, throat
raw from the tail end of a dream
through which your cough and
the smoke of a cigarette sailed. I followed
the deep light of the hallway out

to where the patio roof gaped,
bamboo shades mocking the palm tree
in splintery arpeggios. You stood
flicking ash onto the trampled grass.
I could smell the rain leaving, the sage
enthralled in a bitter virtue for hours.

WATCHING *LAST YEAR AT MARIENBAD* AT ROGER HAGGERTY'S HOUSE IN AUBURN, ALABAMA

There is a corridor of light
through the pines, lint from the Spanish Moss.
There is the fallen sun
like ice and the twit of hidden birds
in our common backyards,
snakes threading the needles.

I walk the block past
Krogers with its exhausted wives
hovering over bins of frozen pork.

No one else has shown but their chairs are here.

We sit flanking the projector.
The opening sequence reminds Roger's
three-year-old daughter
of the wedding cake she ate last week.
It reminds me of my first train in Europe,
the windows, soft implosions
at the entrance of tunnels,
air carving its intricate laces. . . .

The child has fallen asleep with a doll
on the sagging couch.

Here, nothing's mysterious—books and
newspapers. The first time
for anything is the best,
because there is no memory
linking its regrets to drop
like bracelets in the grass. What

a shabby monstrosity spring
actually is! Remember
that park bench, the frail wisteria. . . .

DOG DAYS, JERUSALEM

Exactly at six every evening I go
into the garden to wait for rain.
I'd been told it would come at six
if at all—but the sky goes matte,
so I turn on the sprinklers and follow
the lizard's woven escape
as water falls through itself like pity.

How tiny this broken applause!
In the library, beneath the fluted lamp,
I have set out black tea and oranges—
carefully, though no one will see me.
Night comes in on the clear register
of the *shofar*,
poor relative blowing its children home.

OZONE

> *. . . Does the cosmic*
> *space we dissolve into taste of us, then?*
> —RILKE, *The Second Elegy*

Everything civilized will whistle before
it rages—kettle of the asthmatic,
the aerosol can and its immaculate awl
perforating the dome of heaven.

We wire the sky for comfort;
we thread it through our lungs for a perfect fit.
We've arranged this calm, though it is constantly
unraveling.

> *Where does it go then,*
> *atmosphere suckered up*
> *an invisible flue?*
> *How can we know where it goes?*

A gentleman pokes blue through a buttonhole.

> *Rising, the pulse*
> *sings:*
> *memento mei*

The sky is wired so it won't fall down.
Each house notches into its neighbor
and then the next, the whole row scaldingly white,
unmistakable as a set of bared teeth.

> *to pull the plug*
> *to disappear into an empty bouquet*

If only we could lose ourselves
in the wreckage of the moment! Forget
where we stand, dead center, and
look up, look up,
track a falling star . . .

> now you see it

> now you don't

TURNING THIRTY, I CONTEMPLATE STUDENTS BICYCLING HOME

This is the weather of change
and clear light. This is
weather on its B side,
askew, that propels
the legs of young men
in tight jeans wheeling

through the tired, wise
spring. Crickets too
awake in choirs
out of sight, although

I imagine we see
the same thing
and for a long way.

This, then, weather
to start over.
Evening rustles
her skirts of sulky
organza. Skin
prickles, defining
what is and shall not be. . . .

How private
the complaint of these
green hills.

PARTICULARS

She discovered she felt better
if the simplest motions
had their origin in agenda—
second coffee at nine or eating just
the top half of the muffin, no butter
with blueberry jam. She caught herself
crying every morning, ten sharp, as if
the weather front had swerved,
a titanic low pressure system
moving in as night steamed off
and left a day with nothing else
to fill it but moisture. She wept
steadily, and once
she recognized the pattern,
took care to be in one spot waiting
a few moments before. They weren't
tears of relief, and after a few weeks
not even of a particular sorrow.
*We never learn a secret until
it's useless,* she thought, and perhaps

that was what she was weeping over:
the lack of conclusion,
the eternal *dénouement.*

YOUR DEATH

On the day that will always belong to you,
lunar clockwork had faltered
and I was certain. Walking
the streets of Manhattan I thought:
Remember this day. I felt already
like an urn, filling with wine.

To celebrate, your son and I
took a stroll through Bloomingdale's
where he developed a headache
among the copper skillets and
tiers of collapsible baskets.
Pain tracked us through
the china, driving us
finally to the subway
and home,

where the phone was ringing
with bad news. Even now,
my new daughter
asleep in the crib, I can't shake
the moment his headache stopped
and the day changed ownership.
I felt robbed. Even the first
bite of the tuna fish sandwich
I had bought at the corner
became yours.

THE WAKE

Your absence distributed itself
like an invitation.
Friends and relatives
kept coming, trying
to fill up the house.
But the rooms still gaped—
the green hanger swang empty, and
the head of the table
demanded a plate.

When I sat down in the armchair
your warm breath fell
over my shoulder.
When I climbed to bed I walked
through your blind departure.
The others stayed downstairs,
trying to cover
the silence with weeping.

When I lay down between the sheets
I lay down in the cool waters
of my own womb
and became the child
inside, innocuous
as a button, helplessly growing.
I slept because it was the only
thing I could do. I even dreamed.
I couldn't stop myself.

III

*Where's a word, a
talisman, to hold
against the world?*

THE OTHER SIDE OF THE HOUSE

But it wasn't a dream; it was a place! And you
. . . and you . . . and you . . . and you were there!
—DOROTHY, in *The Wizard of Oz*

I walk out the kitchen door
trailing extension cords into the open
gaze of the Southwest—

the green surreptitious,
dusty like a trenchcoat.

From the beautiful lawnmower
float curls of evaporated gasoline;
the hinged ax of the butterfly pauses.

Where am I in the stingy
desert broom, where
in the blank soul of the olive?
I hear the sand preparing to flee. . . .

Many still moments,
aligned, repair
the thin split of an afternoon—
its orange fiction, the dim
aggression of my daughter on the terrace drawing
her idea of a home. Somewhere

I learned to walk out of a thought
and not snap back the way
railroad cars telescope into a train.

The sand flies so fast, it leaves no shadow.

PASTORAL

Like an otter, but warm,
she latched onto the shadowy tip
and I watched, diminished
by those amazing gulps. Finished
she let her head loll, eyes
unfocused and large: milk-drunk.

I liked afterwards best, lying
outside on a quilt, her new skin
spread out like meringue. I felt then
what a young man must feel
with his first love asleep on his breast:
desire, and the freedom to imagine it.

HORSE AND TREE

Everybody who's anybody longs to be a tree—
or ride one, hair blown to froth.
That's why horses were invented, and saddles
tooled with singular stars.

This is why we braid their harsh manes
as if they were children, why children
might fear a carousel at first for the way
it insists that life is round. No,

we reply, there is music and then it stops;
the beautiful is always rising and falling.
We call and the children sing back *one more time*.
In the tree the luminous sap ascends.

THE BREATHING, THE ENDLESS NEWS

Every god is lonely, an exile
composed of parts: elk horn,
cloven hoof. Receptacle

for wishes, each god is empty
without us, penitent,
raking our yards into windblown piles. . . .

Children know this: they are
the trailings of gods. Their eyes
hold nothing at birth then fill slowly

with the myth of ourselves. Not so the dolls,
out for the count, each toe pouting from
the slumped-over toddler clothes:

no blossoming there. So we
give our children dolls, and
they know just what to do—

line them up and shoot them.
With every execution
doll and god grow stronger.

AFTER READING *MICKEY IN*
THE NIGHT KITCHEN FOR THE
THIRD TIME BEFORE BED
I'm in the milk and the milk's in me! . . . I'm Mickey!

My daughter spreads her legs
to find her vagina:
hairless, this mistaken
bit of nomenclature
is what a stranger cannot touch
without her yelling. She demands
to see mine and momentarily

we're a lopsided star
among the spilled toys,
my prodigious scallops
exposed to her neat cameo.

And yet the same glazed
tunnel, layered sequences.
She is three; that makes this
innocent. *We're pink!*
she shrieks, and bounds off.

Every month she wants
to know where it hurts
and what the wrinkled string means
between my legs. *This is good blood*
I say, but that's wrong, too.
How to tell her that it's what makes us—
black mother, cream child.
That we're in the pink
and the pink's in us.

GENETIC EXPEDITION

Each evening I see my breasts
slacker, black-tipped
like the heavy plugs on hot water bottles;
each day resembling more the spiked fruits
dangling from natives in the *National Geographic*
my father forbade us to read.

Each morning I drip coffee onto my blouse
and tear into one slice of German bread,
thin layer of margarine, radishes, the years
spreading across my dark behind, even more
sumptuous after childbirth, the part of me
I swore to relish

always. My child has
her father's hips, his hair
like the miller's daughter, combed gold.
Though her lips are mine, housewives
stare when we cross the parking lot
because of that ghostly profusion.

You can't be cute, she says. *You're big.*
She's lost her toddler's belly,
that seaworthy prow. She regards me
with serious eyes, power-lit,
atomic gaze
I'm sucked into, sheer through to

the gray brain of sky.

BACKYARD, 6 A.M.

Nudged by bees, morning brightens to detail:
purple trumpets of the sage dropped
to the floor of the world. I'm back
home, jet lag and laundry,
space stapled down with every step. . . .

I swore to be good and the plane didn't
fall out of the sky. Is there such a thing
as a warning? I swear

I hear wings, and spiders
quickening in the forgotten shrines,
unwinding
each knot of grief,
each snagged insistence.

IV

I know the dark delight of being strange,
The penalty of difference in the crowd,
The loneliness of wisdom among fools . . .

—CLAUDE MCKAY

DEDICATION

after Czeslaw Milosz

Ignore me. This request is knotted—
I'm not ashamed to admit it.
I won't promise anything. I am a magic
that can deafen you like a rainstorm or a well.

I am clear on introductions, the five minute flirt,
the ending of old news.
Broken color, this kind of wanting,
its tawdriness, its awkward uncertainties.

Once there was a hill thick with red maples
and a small brook
emerging from black briars.
There was quiet: no wind
to snatch the cries of birds flung above
where I sat and didn't know you yet.

What are music or books if not ways
to trap us in rumors? The freedom of fine cages!
I did not want bad music, I did not want
faulty scholarship; I wanted only to know

what I had missed, early on—
that ironic half-salute of the truly lost.

ARS POETICA

Thirty miles to the only decent restaurant
was nothing, a blink
in the long dull stare of Wyoming.
Halfway there the unknown but terribly
important essayist yelled Stop!
I wanna be *in* this; and walked
fifteen yards onto the land
before sky bore down and he came running,
crying Jesus—there's nothing out there!

I once met an Australian novelist
who told me he never learned to cook
because it robbed creative energy.
What he wanted most was
to be mute; he stacked up pages;
he entered each day with an ax.

What I want is this poem to be small,
a ghost town
on the larger map of wills.
Then you can pencil me in as a hawk:
a traveling x-marks-the-spot.

ARROW

The eminent scholar "took the bull by the horns,"
substituting urban black speech for the voice
of an illiterate cop in Aristophanes' *Thesmophoriazusae*.
And we sat there.
Dana's purple eyes deepened, Becky
twitched to her hairtips
and Janice in her red shoes
scribbled *he's an arsch loch; do you want*
to leave? He's a model product of his
education, I scribbled back; *we can learn from this.*

So we sat through the applause
and my chest flashed hot, a void
sucking at my guts until I was all
flamed surface. I would have to speak up.
Then the scholar progressed

to his prize-winning translations of
the Italian Nobel Laureate. He explained the poet
to us: immense difficulty
with human relationships; sensitive;
women were a scrim through which he could see
heaven.

We sat through it. Quite lovely, these poems.
We could learn from them although they were saying
you women are nothing, nothing at all.

When the moment came I raised my hand,
phrased my question as I had to: sardonic,
eminently civil my condemnation
phrased in the language of fathers—
felt the room freeze behind me.
And the answer came as it had to:
humanity—celebrate our differences—
the virility of ethnicity. My students
sat there already devising

their different ways of coping:
Dana knowing it best to have
the migraine at once, get the poison out quickly
Becky holding it back for five hours   and Janice
making it to the evening reading
and party afterwards
in black pants and tunic with silver mirrors
her shoes pointed and studded, wicked witch shoes:
Janice who will wear red for three days or
yellow brighter
than her hair so she can't be
seen   at all

STITCHES

When skin opens
where a scar
should be, I think nothing but
"So I *am* white underneath!"
Blood swells then
dribbles into the elbow.

All that preparation for nothing!
I phone the university

to explain. My husband
storms in, motor running,
pales, and packs me off to Emergency.

Wear a red dress for the first time
in a year, and look what happens.
You were on your way to class,
you had a plane to catch after—
the bulging suitcase knocked you off-center.

The doctor's teeth are beavery, yellow:
he whistles as he works, as topsoil
puckers over its wound. Amazing
there's no pain—just pressure
as the skin's tugged up by his thread

like a trout, a black line straight
from a seamstress' nightmare: foot-tread
pedaling the needle right through.

You just can't stop being witty, can you?

Oh, but I can. I always could.

IN THE MUSEUM

a boy, at most
sixteen.

Besieged by the drums
and flags of youth,
brilliant gravity
and cornucopian stone

retreat.

The Discus Thrower
(reproduction)
stares as he crosses the lobby
and enters
the XIVth century.

I follow him as far
as the room with the blue Madonnas.

AND COUNTING

(*Bellagio, Italy*)

Well of course I'm not worth it but neither is
the Taj Mahal for that matter so who's counting?
Someone's got to listen to the fountain;
someone is due to catch the *nymphaea tuberosa*
closing promptly five till five. Opulence
breathes on its own a little better
if there's a gardener raking or a scholar
primed to record its suscitation. I came here

to write, knock a few poems off the ledger
of accounts payable—only to discover
pasta put me under just as neatly as sambuca
would catapult me into telepathic communication. So
I took a few day trips, sprained an ankle on the courts,
fell asleep over Catullus-*cum*-Zukofsky . . . in

short, nothing happened that wasn't unexceptional,
but that's the crux of moral implication, is it not?
Mother Mary, ingénue with the golden womb,
you would not comprehend how cruel a modern game of
tennis is: you only had one phosphorescent ball.
Here's a riddle for Our Age: when the sky's the limit,
how can you tell you've gone too far?

DIALECTICAL ROMANCE

He asked if she believed in God
so she looked him in the eye
before answering No but he wouldn't
give in: Not even a little bit?
Then because it was raining and
they were walking down a path others
might have called paradise, she added
Not even a little—though at times
she wished she could. It was a lie
but she was being polite; besides,
they had just turned from Suicide Point
and it seemed the social thing to say.

He believed there was a force but didn't feel
compelled to give it a name; it needn't be
embodied. She thought of the Virgin
at Bergamo, marble limbs dressed in dusty
crinolines, a life-sized Barbie doll.

Some force has to have made all this—
his armsweep sending more droplets down,
gravel protesting like gritting teeth—
and then set everything loose in it.

So God's given up? she ventured, which made him
swallow. Remembering where they'd been, then,
those soaked crags and lake-stunned altitudes,
she dredged up for his sake a comparison
from computers: a program so large
there could be no answer
except in working it through.

MEDUSA

I've got to go
down where my eye
can't reach
hairy star
who forgets to shiver
forgets the cool suck
inside

Someday long
off someone will
see me
fling me up
until I hook
into sky

drop his memory

My hair
dry water

IN A NEUTRAL CITY

Someday we'll talk about the day lily,
the puff dandelion aloof on its milky stalk,
wild birds defying notation. Someday
the last sad trickle in a toilet stall
will recall fountains sighing into themselves
and ant-freckled stones
swept clean with a breath. In rain

over lunch we will search for a topic
only to remember a hill, a path hushed
in the waxen shade of magnolias.
Someday we'll talk because there'll be
little else to say:
and then the cheese and pears will arrive,
and the worms.

V

Don't hope for an elsewhere.
Now that you've wasted your life here, in this small corner,
You've wasted it everywhere in the world.

—CAVAFY

SAINTS

She used to pull them
from herself and count:
Have mercy, have mercy—
blackeyed peas flicked into a pot.

Why go out into the sunshine
and blustery azaleas, why leave
this overcrowded bed?
She's fat now, she stinks in warm weather.
She'll pin on a hat, groan into a pew,
spend the hour watching stained glass
swirl through Michael's boat
like holy water.

Between her knees, each had been
a neat hunger,
each one a freedom.
So many now, perishing under the rafters!
They are like the tin replicas of eyes and limbs
hung up in small churches,
meticulous
cages, medallions
swinging in the dazed air.

GENIE'S PRAYER UNDER THE KITCHEN SINK

> *Housebuilding was conceived as a heroic
> effort to stop time, suspend decay and inter-
> rupt the ordained flow to ruin that started
> with Adam's fall.*
> —from *House* by TRACY KIDDER

Hair and bacon grease, pearl button
popped in the search for a shawl, smashed radiant aluminum
foil, blunt shreds of wax paper—
nothing gets lost, you can't flush the shit
without it floating back in the rheumy eye of the bowl

or coagulating in the drop-belly of transitional pipes.
And who gets to drag his bad leg
into the kitchen and under the sink,
flashlight scattering roaches, rusted brillo pads
his earned divan?

                    The hot water squeezed
to a trickle so she counted out the finger holes
and dialed her least-loved son.
I don't believe in stepping
in the goddam shoes of any other man
but I came because I'm good at this, I'm good

with my hands; last March I bought some 2 by 4s
at Home Depot and honed them down
to the sleekest, blondest, free-standing bar
any mildewed basement in a cardboard housing tract
under the glass gloom of a factory clock
ever saw. I put the best bottles
behind it: Dimple scotch, crystal Gordon,
one mean nigger rye. I stacked the records.
Called two girls who like to perform on shag rugs,
spun my mirrored globe and watched.

They were sweet, like pet monkeys. I know
Mom called me over so I'd have to lurch up
the porch steps and she could click her tongue
and say, That's what you get for evil living. Christ,
she took in wash through fourteen children and
he left her every time, went off on a 9-month binge
while the ripening babies ate her rich thighs
to sticks.

                I was the last one; I'm Genie,
Eugene June Bug; the others made me
call them "Aunt" and "Uncle" in public.
All except Annalee—cancer screwed *her*.
She withered like my leg. She dragged her body
through the house like a favorite doll.

Yes, I'm a man born too late for
Ain't-that-a-shame, I'm a monkey
with a message and a heart like
my father who fell laughing to his knees
when it burst and 24 crows spilled
from his mouth and they were all named Jim.

When I'm finished here
I'm gonna build a breezeway next,
with real nice wicker on some astroturf.

THE GORGE

I.

Little Cuyahoga's done up left town.
No one saw it leaving.
No one saw it leaving

Though it left a twig or two,
And a snaky line of rotting
Fish, a dead man's shoes,

Gnats, scarred pocket-
Books, a rusted garden nozzle,
Rats and crows. April

In bone and marrow. Soaked
With sugary dogwood, the gorge floats
In the season's morass,

Remembering its walnut, its hickory,
Its oak, its elm,
Its sassafras. Ah,

II.

April's arthritic magnitude!
Little Joe ran away
From the swollen man

On the porch, ran across
The muck to the railroad track.
Lost his penny and sat

Right down by the rail,
There where his father
Couldn't see him crying.

That's why the express
Stayed on the track.
That's why a man

On a porch shouted out
Because his son forgot
His glass of iced water. That's

Why they carried little Joe
Home and why his toe
Ain't never coming back. Oh

III.

This town reeks mercy.
This gorge leaves a trail
Of anecdotes,

The poor man's history.

CANARY

for Michael S. Harper

Billie Holiday's burned voice
had as many shadows as lights,
a mournful candelabra against a sleek piano,
the gardenia her signature under that ruined face.

(Now you're cooking, drummer to bass,
magic spoon, magic needle.
Take all day if you have to
with your mirror and your bracelet of song.)

Fact is, the invention of women under siege
has been to sharpen love in the service of myth.

If you can't be free, be a mystery.

THE ISLAND WOMEN OF PARIS

skim from curb to curb like regatta,
from Pont Neuf to the Quai de la Rappe
in cool negotiation with traffic,
each a country to herself
transposed to this city
by a fluke called "imperial courtesy."

The island women glide past held aloft
by a wire running straight to heaven.
Who can ignore their ornamental bearing,
turbans haughty as parrots,
or deft braids carved into airy cages
transfixed on their manifest brows?

The island women move through Paris
as if they had just finished inventing

their destinations. It's better
not to get in their way. And better
not look an island woman in the eye—
unless you like feeling unnecessary.

À L'OPÉRA

A friend, blonde pigtail flung over an ear,
consoles her with cheek kisses.
They take no notice of the police
ranged down the steps in two lanes
from the marbled interior
where a delegation is
happening—someone famous, perhaps.

More friends arrive. Of them the boys,
correct in their flannels, kiss her too,
and with the ironic grace of the French
take her briefly to their chests.

Now the police block off the boulevard,
traffic snorting at their backs;
and though I wait for fifteen minutes
in the doorway of a corner café
no dignitary ever descends,
nor does she stop crying.

OBBLIGATO

*Consider that I have loved you for forty-nine years, that I have loved you since
childhood despite the storms that have wasted my life. . . . I have loved you. I
love you and will continue to love you, and I am sixty-one years old, I know
the world and have no illusions.*
   —HECTOR BERLIOZ to Madame F.

Patrons talk and talk and nothing
comes. His thighs shift, the cup flies

sending dish and creamed tea
spinning, a corona of perfect disgrace.

The murmured solicitudes, the gloves.

He could debate the existence of God, describe
the vexed look on the face of the timpanist
who had never heard of felt-tips. Or the trumpets
failing their entrance in *Iphegenie*—

I fear I suffer from poplar blossoms,
so profuse this season.

The entire summer he was twelve she wore pink shoes.

Invisible command, the enemy everywhere.

LINT

Beneath the brushed wing of the mallard
an awkward loveliness.

Under the cedar lid a mirror
and a box in a box.

Blue is all around
like an overturned bowl.

What to do with this noise
and persistent lint,

the larder filled past caring?
How good to revolve

on the edge of a system—
small, unimaginable, cold.

THE ROYAL WORKSHOPS

1

Stone kettles on the beach by Sidon.
Salt and slime, colorless juice:
murex brandaris,
murex trunculus,
simmering.

Two kettles
on the salt beach:
dark red,
dark blue.

2

By the sign of his hand
you shall know him, holy slave.
By the litmus mark on his earlobe
you shall know the Jew, the wretched dyer.

3

Zebulun wails:
I received only mountains &
hills, oceans & rivers.

God replies:
Because of the purple snail
all will be in need of your service.

Zebulun says:
You gave my brother countries;
me you gave the snail.

God answers:
After all, I made them dependent on you
for the snail.

4

A slave practised in the labor
of red-purple and blue

was sent from Tyre to the Temple
to ferment an unpierceable scrim.

5

The Romans had their Jews,
the Greeks their Abyssinians—
red-haired Thaddaeus,
blue-skinned Muhammed.

6

Slave's work, to wring and dry and drape;
man's work to adorn the unspeakable.
Evening lavishes shade on a cold battlefield
as God retreats

before a fanfare of trumpets and heliotrope.

ON THE ROAD TO DAMASCUS

*And it came to pass, that, as I made my
journey, and was come nigh unto Damascus
about noon, suddenly there shone from heaven
a great light round about me. And I fell to the
ground . . .*

ACTS 22:6–7

They say I was struck down by the voice of an angel:
    flames poured through the radiant fabric of heaven
as I cried out and fell to my knees.

My first recollection was of Unbroken Blue—
    but two of the guards have already sworn by
the tip of my tongue set ablaze. As an official,

I recognize the lure of a good story:
    useless to suggest that my mount
had stumbled, that I was pitched into a clump

of wild chamomile, its familiar stink
　　soothing even as my palms sprang blisters
under the nicked leaves. I heard shouts,

the horse pissing in terror—but my eyes
　　had dropped to my knees, and I saw nothing.
I was a Roman and had my business

among the clouded towers of Damascus.
　　I had not counted on earth rearing,
honey streaming down a parched sky,

a spear skewering me to the dust of the road
　　on the way to the city I would never
enter now, her markets steaming with vendors

and compatriots in careless armor lifting a hand
　　in greeting as they call out my name,
only to find no one home.

OLD FOLK'S HOME, JERUSALEM
for Harry Timar

Evening, the bees fled, the honeysuckle
in its golden dotage, all the sickrooms ajar.
Law of the Innocents: What doesn't end, sloshes over . . .
even here, where destiny girds the cucumber.

So you wrote a few poems. The horned
thumbnail hooked into an ear doesn't care.
The gray underwear wadded over a belt says So what.

The night air is minimalist,
a needlepoint with raw moon as signature.
In this desert the question's not
Can you see? but *How far off?*

Valley settlements put on their lights
like armor; there's finch chit and my sandal's
inconsequential crunch.

Everyone waiting here was once in love.

MOTHER LOVE

(1995)

AN INTACT WORLD

"Sonnet" literally means "little song." The sonnet is a *heile Welt*, an intact world where everything is in sync, from the stars down to the tiniest mite on a blade of grass. And if the "true" sonnet reflects the music of the spheres, it then follows that any variation from the strictly Petrarchan or Shakespearean forms represents a world gone awry.

Or does it? Can't form also be a talisman against disintegration? The sonnet defends itself against the vicissitudes of fortune by its charmed structure, its beautiful bubble. All the while, though, chaos is lurking outside the gate.

The ancient story of Demeter and Persephone is just such a tale of a violated world. It is a modern dilemma as well—there comes a point when a mother can no longer protect her child, when the daughter must go her own way into womanhood. Persephone, out picking flowers with her girlfriends, wanders off from the group. She has just stooped to pluck a golden narcissus, when the earth opens and Hades emerges, dragging her down with him into the Underworld. Inconsolable in her grief, Demeter neglects her duties as goddess of agriculture, and the crops wither. The Olympians disapprove of the abduction but are more shaken by Demeter's reaction, her refusal to return to her godly work in defiance of the laws of nature; she's even left her throne in Olympus and taken to wandering about on earth disguised as a mortal. In varying degrees she is admonished or pitied by the other gods for the depth of her grief. She refuses to accept her fate, however; she strikes out against the Law, forcing Zeus to ask his brother Hades to return Persephone to her mother. Hades agrees.

But ah, can we ever really go back home, as if nothing had happened? Before returning to the surface, the girl eats a few pomegranate seeds, not realizing that anyone who partakes of the food of the dead cannot be wholly restored to the living. So she must spend half of each year at Hades' side, as Queen of the Underworld, and her mother must acquiesce: every fall and winter Demeter is permitted to grieve for the loss of her daughter, letting vegetation wilt and die, but she is obliged to act cheerful in spring and summer, making the earth blossom and bear fruit.

Sonnets seemed the proper mode for most of this work—and not only in homage and as counterpoint to Rilke's *Sonnets to Orpheus*. Much has been said about the many ways to "violate" the sonnet in the service of American speech or modern love or whatever; I will simply say that I like how the sonnet comforts even while its prim borders (but what a pretty fence!) are stultifying; one is constantly bumping up against Order. The Demeter/Persephone cycle of betrayal and regeneration is ideally suited for this form since all three—mother-goddess, daughter-consort and poet—are struggling to sing in their chains.

RITA DOVE

I

One had to choose,
and who would choose the horror?

—JAMES HILLMAN,
The Dream and the Underworld

HEROES

A flower in a weedy field:
make it a poppy. You pick it.
Because it begins to wilt

you run to the nearest house
to ask for a jar of water.
The woman on the porch starts

screaming: you've plucked the last poppy
in her miserable garden, the one
that gave her the strength every morning

to rise! It's too late for apologies
though you go through the motions, offering
trinkets and a juicy spot in the written history

she wouldn't live to read, anyway.
So you strike her, she hits
her head on a white boulder,

and there's nothing to be done
but break the stone into gravel
to prop up the flower in the stolen jar

you have to take along,
because you're a fugitive now
and you can't leaves clues.

Already the story's starting to unravel,
the villagers stirring as your heart
pounds into your throat. O why

did you pick that idiot flower?
Because it was the last one
and you knew

it was going to die.

II

Baby, baby, if he hears you
As he gallops past the house,
Limb from limb at once he'll tear you,
Just as pussy tears a mouse.

And he'll beat you, beat you, beat you,
And he'll beat you all to pap,
And he'll eat you, eat you, eat you,
Every morsel snap, snap, snap.

—MOTHER GOOSE

PRIMER

In the sixth grade I was chased home by
the Gatlin kids, three skinny sisters
in rolled-down bobby socks. Hissing
Brainiac! and *Mrs. Stringbean!*, they trod my heel.
I knew my body was no big deal
but never thought to retort: who's
calling *who* skinny? (Besides, I knew
they'd beat me up.) I survived
their shoves across the schoolyard
because my five-foot-zero mother drove up
in her Caddie to shake them down to size.
Nothing could get me into that car.
I took the long way home, swore
I'd show them all: I would grow up.

PARTY DRESS FOR A FIRST BORN

Headless girl so ill at ease on the bed,
I know, if you could, what you're thinking of:
nothing. I used to think that, too,
whenever I sat down to a full plate
or unwittingly stepped on an ant.
When I ran to my mother, waiting radiant
as a cornstalk at the edge of the field,
nothing else mattered: the world stood still.

Tonight men stride like elegant scissors across the lawn
to the women arrayed there, petals waiting to loosen.
When I step out, disguised in your blushing skin,
they will nudge each other to get a peek
and I will smile, all the while wishing them dead.
Mother's calling. Stand up: it will be our secret.

PERSEPHONE, FALLING

One narcissus among the ordinary beautiful
flowers, one unlike all the others! She pulled,
stooped to pull harder—
when, sprung out of the earth
on his glittering terrible
carriage, he claimed his due.
It is finished. No one heard her.
No one! She had strayed from the herd.

(Remember: go straight to school.
This is important, stop fooling around!
Don't answer to strangers. Stick
with your playmates. Keep your eyes down.)
This is how easily the pit
opens. This is how one foot sinks into the ground.

THE SEARCH

Blown apart by loss, she let herself go—
wandered the neighborhood hatless, breasts
swinging under a ratty sweater, crusted
mascara blackening her gaze. It was a shame,
the wives whispered, to carry on so.
To them, wearing foam curlers arraigned
like piglets to market was almost debonair,
but an uncombed head?—not to be trusted.

The men watched more closely, tantalized
by so much indifference. Winter came early and still
she frequented the path by the river until
one with murmurous eyes pulled her down to size.
Sniffed Mrs. Franklin, ruling matron, to the rest:
Serves her right, the old mare.

PROTECTION

Are you having a good time?
Are you having a time at all?
Everywhere in the garden I see the slim vine
of your neck, the stubborn baby curls . . .

I know I'm not saying this right.
"Good" hair has no body
in this country; like trained ivy,
it hangs and shines. Mine comes out

in clusters. Is there such
a thing as a warning? The Hawaiian
mulberry is turning to ash

and the snail has lost its home.
Are you really all over with? How done
is gone?

THE NARCISSUS FLOWER

I remember my foot in its frivolous slipper,
a frightened bird . . . not the earth unzipped

but the way I could see my own fingers and hear
myself scream as the blossom incinerated.

And though nothing could chasten
the plunge, this man
adamant as a knife easing into

the humblest crevice, I found myself at
the center of a calm so pure, it was hate.

The mystery is, you can eat fear
before fear eats you,

you can live beyond dying—
and become a queen
whom nothing surprises.

PERSEPHONE ABDUCTED

She cried out for Mama, who did not
hear. She left with a wild eye thrown back,
she left with curses, rage
that withered her features to a hag's.
No one can tell a mother how to act:
there are no laws when laws are broken, no names
to call upon. Some say there's nourishment for pain,

and call it Philosophy.
That's for the birds, vulture and hawk,
the large ones who praise
the miracle of flight because
they use it so diligently.
She left us singing in the field, oblivious
to all but the ache of our own bent backs.

STATISTIC: THE WITNESS

No matter where I turn, she is there
screaming. No matter how
I run, pause to catch a breath—
until I am the one screaming
as the drone of an engine overtakes
the afternoon.

I know I should stop looking, do
as my mother says—turn my head
to the wall and tell Jesus—but
I keep remembering things,
clearer and smaller: his watch,

his wrist, the two ashen ovals
etched on her upturned sandals.

Now I must walk this faithless earth
which cannot readjust an abyss
into flowering meadow.
I will walk until I reach
green oblivion . . . then
I will lie down in its kindness,
in the bottomless lull of her arms.

GRIEF: THE COUNCIL

I told her: enough is enough.
Get a hold on yourself, take a lover,
help some other unfortunate child.

> *to abdicate*
> *to let the garden go to seed*

Yes it's a tragedy, a low-down shame,
but you still got your own life to live. Meanwhile,
ain't nothing we can do but be discreet
and wait. She brightened up a bit, then.
I thought of those blurred snapshots framed
on milk cartons, a new pair each week.

> *soot drifting up from hell*
> *dusting the kale's*
> *green tresses, the corn's green sleeve*

It was pathetic. I bet she ain't took in
a word I said except that last, like
a dog with a chicken bone too greedy to care
if it stick in his gullet and choke him sure.

> *and no design*

I say we gotta see her through.
I say she can't be left too long in that
drafty old house alone.

> *no end-of-day delight*
> *at the creak of the gate*

Sister Jeffries, you could drop in
tomorrow morning, take one
of your Mason jars, something
sweetish, tomatoes or bell peppers.

> *no tender cheek nor ripening grape*
> *destined for wine*

Miz Earl can fetch her later to the movies—
a complicated plot should distract her,
something with a car chase through Manhattan,
loud horns melting to a strings-and-sax ending

> *the last frail tendril snapped free*
> *(though the roots still strain toward her)*

and your basic sunshine pouring through
the clouds. Ain't this crazy weather?
Feels like winter coming on.

> *at last the earth cleared to the sea*
> *at last composure*

MOTHER LOVE

Who can forget the attitude of mothering?
> Toss me a baby and without bothering
to blink I'll catch her, sling him on a hip.
> Any woman knows the remedy for grief
is being needed: duty bugles and we'll
> climb out of exhaustion every time,

bare the nipple or tuck in the sheet,
        heat milk and hum at bedside until
they can dress themselves and rise, primed
        for Love or Glory—those one-way mirrors
girls peer into as their fledgling heroes slip
        through, storming the smoky battlefield.

So when this kind woman approached at the urging
        of her bouquet of daughters
(one for each of the world's corners,
        one for each of the winds to scatter!)
and offered up her only male child for nursing
        (a smattering of flesh, noisy and ordinary),
I put aside the lavish trousseau of the mourner
        for the daintier comfort of pity:
I decided to save him. Each night
        I laid him on the smoldering embers,
sealing his juices in slowly so he might
        be cured to perfection. Oh, I know it
looked damning: at the hearth a muttering crone
        bent over a baby sizzling on a spit
as neat as a Virginia ham. Poor human—
        to scream like that, to make me remember.

BREAKFAST OF CHAMPIONS

Finally, overcast skies. I've crossed a hemisphere,
worked my way through petals and sunlight
to find a place fit for mourning,
a little dust on the laurel branch.
I'll dive into a grateful martini tonight,
eye to eye with the olive adrift in cool ether—
but for now, here's weather to match
my condition: the first pair of Canada geese

have arrived on the lake. I rummage the pantry's
stock for raisins and cereal as they pull
honking out of the mist, a sonic hospital graph
announcing recovery. Arise, it's a brand new morning!
Though I pour myself the recommended bowlful,
stones are what I sprinkle among the chaff.

GOLDEN OLDIE

I made it home early, only to get
stalled in the driveway, swaying
at the wheel like a blind pianist caught in a tune
meant for more than two hands playing.

The words were easy, crooned
by a young girl dying to feel alive, to discover
a pain majestic enough
to live by. I turned the air-conditioning off,

leaned back to float on a film of sweat,
and listened to her sentiment:
Baby, where did our love go?—a lament
I greedily took in

without a clue who my lover
might be, or where to start looking.

III

Who can escape life, fever,
the darkness of the abyss?
lost, lost, lost . . .

—H.D.,
Hermetic Definition

PERSEPHONE IN HELL

I.

I was not quite twenty when I first went down
into the stone chasms of the City of Lights,
every morning four flights creaking under my rubber soles.
At the end of each dim hall, a tiny window tipped
toward the clouds admitted light into
those loveless facilities shared by
the shameful poor and the shamelessly young.
Girded, then, with youth and good tennis shoes,
I climbed down guided
by the smell of bread,
the reek of multiplying yeast.
With my seven words of French,
with my exact change I walked
the storefronts where the double-plated
windows were as coolly arranged
as a spray of bridesmaids:
bazooka sausages, fields of silk,
"ladies' foundations" in winch-and-pulley configurations,

and at last, squadrons of baked goods:
croissants glazed in the sheen of desire,
the sweating dark caps of the *têtes de nègres*,
nipples gleaming on the innocent *beignets*;
I surveyed them, each in its majesty,
and stepped over the tinkling threshold,
instantly foreign: *une baguette et
cinq croissants beurre, s'il vous plait.*
There were five of us, five girls.
Banknote and silver
crossed palms and I was outside again,
awash in a rush of Peugeots and honking
delivery vans.

For a moment I forgot which way to turn,
what the month was, the reason for
my high-pitched vigilance—

then it came back: turn left, cross
the avenue, dodge poodle shit
and tsking nannies. It was October.
Sweat faded into the terried insteps
of my miraculous American sneakers
while the sour ecstasy of bread
(its chaste white wrapper rustling,
the brown heel broken off)
calmed me.

II.

It's an old drama, waiting.
One grows into it,
enough to fill the boredom . . .
it's a treacherous fit.

Mother worried. Mother with her frilly ideals
gave me money to call home every day,
but she couldn't know what I was feeling;
I was doing what she didn't need to know.
I was doing everything and feeling nothing.

corn in the husk
vine unfurling

Autumn soured. Little lace-up boots
appeared on the heels of shopkeepers
while their clientele sported snappier versions;
black parabolas of balcony grills
echoed in their three-inch heels.

my dove   my snail

Two days of rain, how to spend them?
Clip on large earrings, man's sweater, black tights;
walk an old umbrella through the passage
at number 17, dip in for *chocolat chaud*
while watching the Africans
fold up their straw mats and wooden beads.

There was love, of course. Mostly boys:
a flat-faced engineering student from Missouri,
a Texan flaunting his teaspoon of Cherokee blood.
I waited for afterwards—their pale eyelids, foreheads
thrown back so the rapture could evaporate.
I don't believe I was suffering. I was curious, mainly:
How would each one smell, how many ways could he do it?
I was drowning in flowers.

III.

I visited a former schoolmate who'd married
onto the *Île*—a two-room attic walk-up
crammed with mahogany heirlooms,
but just lean over the offensive tin sink in the kitchen
and there she was, Our Lady, crusty with gargoyles.
The party they threw for Armistice Day
was cocktails with bad sculpture,
listening for meaningful conversation
among expatriate Americans lounging against the upright coffins.

> – How're you liking it so far? I admit, you
> gotta dodge shit every place you look.
> – What about them little white poodles
> stamped on sidewalks everywhere? Aren't
> they meant for curbing?
> – Yeah, but Parisians love their dogs too
> much. Besides, Parisians don't mind dog
> shit because it's not their shit, you see; it
> makes them feel superior.

> *are you having a good time*
> *are you having a time at all*

There were crudités, peanuts. Banjos appeared, spilling
zeal like popcorn. I decided to let this party
swing without me.

IV.

Cross the Seine, avoid Our Lady's
crepuscular shadow. Chill at my back.

Which way is bluer?

One round of Boul' Mich: bookstore, kiosk,
heat blast from the metro pit. Down, then.

And if I refuse this being
which way then?

Three stops, out: moonlit façade
of the *Marais*, spun-sugar stucco and iron filigree:
a retinue of little dramas
tucked in for the night.

Through the gutters, dry rivers
of the season's detritus.
Wind soughing the plane trees.
I command my knees to ignore the season
as I scuttle over stones, marking pace
by the intermittent evidence of canine
love: heaped droppings scored with frost.

Near Beaubourg, even the air twitters.
Racks of T-shirts cut from
inferior cloth, postcard stands, all
the assumed élan and bric-a-brac
dissolves with a turn
that pitches me onto the concrete brim
of the Centre Pompidou.

Mon Dieu, the wind!
My head fills with ice.

This is how the pit opens

Sheared of its proletarian stubble
(brothels and cheap hotels),

this bulldozed amphitheater
catches the iron breath of winter, sending
tourist and *clochard* into the breach,
dachshund and snapped umbrella,
each stubborn leaf and exiled twig
swirling into whatever that is
down there, throbbing with neon tubing
like some demented plumber's diagram
of a sinner's soul—

This is how one foot
sinks into the ground

V.

God, humans are a noisy zoo—
especially educated ones armed with *vin rouge*
and an incomprehensible no-act play.

The crush, the unbearable stench!
They insist on overheating these affairs,
as if to remind the leftist bourgeoisie
just who wove those welcome mats
they wipe their combat boots on.
Rad Chic: black corduroy and
leather vests. The saints were right
to flog the body, or starve it into heaven.

I need a *divertissement*:
The next one through that gate,
woman or boy, will get
the full-court press of my ennui.

Merde,
too many at once! Africans,
spilling up the escalator
like oil from lucky soil—

let me get my rules straight.
Should I count them as singular
plural, like popcorn?

Or can I wait for one person
to separate from the crowd,
chin lifted for courage, as if to place
her brave, lost countenance
under my care . . .

Contact.

VI.

After the wind, this air
imploded down my throat,
a hot, rank syrup swirled with smoke
from a hundred cigarettes.
Soft chatter roaring. French nothings.
I don't belong here.

> She doesn't belong, that's certain.
> Leather skirt's slipped
> a bit: sweet. No gloves? American,
> because she wears black badly.
> I'd like to see her in chartreuse,
> walking around like a living
> after-dinner drink.

He inclines his head, rather massive,
like a cynical parrot. Almost a smile.

> *"Puis-je vous offrir mes services?"*

Sotto voce, his inquiry
curls down to lick my hand.
Standard nicety, probably,
but my French could not stand up
to meet it.

> *"Or myself, if you are looking."*
> I whisper this. I'm sure she doesn't understand.

"Pardon me?"

"Excuse, I thought you were French.
You are looking for someone?"

"Yes, I'm . . . sure he's here somewhere."
Here you are.

"I hope he won't let himself
be found too soon. A drink?"

He's gone and back, as easily as smoke,
in each hand a slim glass
alive with a brilliant lime.
"What time is it?"

she blurts,
shrinking from the glass.
"*À minuit.* Midnight.
The zero hour,
you call it?"

Again the dark smile.
"Some call it that."

"Chartreuse," I say, holding out a glass,
"is a tint not to be found *au naturel*
in all of France, except in bottles
and certain days at the Côte d'Azur
when sun performs on ocean what
we call *un mirage*, a—"

"trick of light." I take the glass,
lift it to meet his.

VII.

if I whispered to the moon

if I whispered to the olive

which would hear me?

the garden gone

the city around me

it was cold I entered

I entered for warmth

a part of me had been waiting

already in this cold longing

who has lost me?

be still, mother whispers

and let sorrow travel

be still she whispers

and light will enter

I am waiting

you are on the way

I am listening

the seed in darkness

I am waiting

you rise into my arms

I part the green sheaths

I part the brown field

and you are sinking

through heat the whispers

through whispers the sighing

through sighing the darkness

I am waiting

you are on your way

IV

On and on my mother would go. No small part of my life was so unimportant that she hadn't made a note of it, and now she would tell it to me over and over again.

—JAMAICA KINCAID,
"The Circling Hand"

HADES' PITCH

If I could just touch your ankle, he whispers, *there*
on the inside, above the bone—leans closer,
breath of lime and peppers—*I know I could*
make love to you. She considers
this, secretly thrilled, though she wasn't quite
sure what he meant. He was good
with words, words that went straight to the liver.
Was she falling for him out of sheer boredom—
cooped up in this anything-but-humble dive, stone
gargoyles leering and brocade drapes licked with fire?
Her ankle burns where he described it. She sighs
just as her mother aboveground stumbles, is caught
by the fetlock—bereft in an instant—
while the Great Man drives home his desire.

WIEDERKEHR

He only wanted me for happiness:
to walk in air
and not think so much,
to watch the smile
begun in his eyes
end on the lips
his eyes caressed.

He merely hoped, in darkness, to smell
rain; and though he saw how still
I sat to hold the rain untouched
inside me, he never asked
if I would stay. Which is why,
when the choice appeared,
I reached for it.

WIRING HOME

Lest the wolves loose their whistles
and shopkeepers inquire,

keep moving; though your knees flush
red as two chapped apples,

keep moving, head up,
past the beggar's cold cup,

past fires banked under chestnuts
and the trumpeting kiosk's

tales of odyssey and heartbreak
until, turning a corner, you stand

staring: ambushed
by a window of canaries

bright as a thousand
golden narcissi.

THE BISTRO STYX

She was thinner, with a mannered gauntness
as she paused just inside the double
glass doors to survey the room, silvery cape
billowing dramatically behind her. *What's this,*

I thought, lifting a hand until
she nodded and started across the parquet;
that's when I saw she was dressed all in gray,
from a kittenish cashmere skirt and cowl

down to the graphite signature of her shoes.
"Sorry I'm late," she panted, though
she wasn't, sliding into the chair, her cape

tossed off in a shudder of brushed steel.
We kissed. Then I leaned back to peruse
my blighted child, this wary aristocratic mole.

"How's business?" I asked, and hazarded
a motherly smile to keep from crying out:
Are you content to conduct your life
as a cliché and, what's worse,

an anachronism, the brooding artist's demimonde?
Near the rue Princesse they had opened
a gallery *cum* souvenir shop which featured
fuzzy off-color Monets next to his acrylics, no doubt,

plus bearded African drums and the occasional miniature
gargoyle from Notre Dame the Great Artist had
carved at breakfast with a pocket knife.

"Tourists love us. The Parisians, of course"—
she blushed—"are amused, though not without
a certain admiration . . ."
                              The Chateaubriand

arrived on a bone-white plate, smug and absolute
in its fragrant crust, a black plug steaming
like the heart plucked from the chest of a worthy enemy;
one touch with her fork sent pink juices streaming.

"Admiration for what?" Wine, a bloody
Pinot Noir, brought color to her cheeks. "Why,
the aplomb with which we've managed
to support our Art"—meaning he'd convinced

her to pose nude for his appalling canvases,
faintly futuristic landscapes strewn
with carwrecks and bodies being chewed

by rabid cocker spaniels. "I'd like to come by
the studio," I ventured, "and see the new stuff."
"Yes, if you wish . . ." A delicate rebuff

before the warning: "He dresses all
in black now. Me, he drapes in blues and carmine—
and even though I think it's kinda cute,
in company I tend toward more muted shades."

She paused and had the grace
to drop her eyes. She did look ravishing,
spookily insubstantial, a lipstick ghost on tissue,
or as if one stood on a fifth-floor terrace

peering through a fringe of rain at Paris'
dreaming chimney pots, each sooty issue
wobbling skyward in an ecstatic oracular spiral.

"And he never thinks of food. I wish
I didn't have to plead with him to eat. . . ." Fruit
and cheese appeared, arrayed on leaf-green dishes.

I stuck with café crème. "This Camembert's
so ripe," she joked, "it's practically grown hair,"
mucking a golden glob complete with parsley sprig
onto a heel of bread. Nothing seemed to fill

her up: She swallowed, sliced into a pear,
speared each tear-shaped lavaliere
and popped the dripping mess into her pretty mouth.
Nowhere the bright tufted fields, weighted

vines and sun poured down out of the south.
"But are you happy?" Fearing, I whispered it
quickly. "What? You know, Mother"—

she bit into the starry rose of a fig—
"one really should try the fruit here."
I've lost her, I thought, and called for the bill.

V

Tighten the sails of night as far as you can,
for the daylight cannot carry me.

—KADIA MOLODOWSKY,
"White Night"

BLUE DAYS

Under pressure Mick tells me one
of the jokes truckers pass among themselves: *Why
do women have legs?* I can't imagine;
the day is too halcyon, beyond the patio too Arizonan
blue, sparrows drunk on figs and the season's first corn
stacked steaming on the wicker table. . . . *I
give up; why do they?* As if I weren't one
of "them." Nothing surpasses these
kernels, taut-to-bursting sweet,
tiny rows translucent as baby teeth.
Remember, you asked for it:
to keep them from tracking slime over the floor.

Demeter, here's another one for your basket
of mysteries.

NATURE'S ITINERARY

Irene says it's the altitude
that makes my period late;
this time, though, it's eluded
me entirely. I shouldn't worry (I'm medically regulated)
—but hell, I brought these thirty sanitary pads
all the way from Köln to Mexico, prepared
for more than metaphorical bloodletting among the glad rags
of the Festival Internacional de Poesía,
and I forbid
my body to be so cavalier.
Taking the pill is like using a safety net
but then, beforehand, having a beer—
a man's invention to numb us so we
can't tell which way the next wind's blowing.

SONNET IN PRIMARY COLORS

This is for the woman with one black wing
perched over her eyes: lovely Frida, erect
among parrots, in the stern petticoats of the peasant,
who painted herself a present—
wildflowers entwining the plaster corset
her spine resides in, that flaming pillar—
this priestess in the romance of mirrors.

Each night she lay down in pain and rose
to the celluloid butterflies of her Beloved Dead,
Lenin and Marx and Stalin arrayed at the footstead.
And rose to her easel, the hundred dogs panting
like children along the graveled walks of the garden, Diego's
love a skull in the circular window
of the thumbprint searing her immutable brow.

DEMETER MOURNING

Nothing can console me. You may bring silk
to make skin sigh, dispense yellow roses
in the manner of ripened dignitaries.
You can tell me repeatedly
I am unbearable (and I know this):
still, nothing turns the gold to corn,
nothing is sweet to the tooth crushing in.

I'll not ask for the impossible;
one learns to walk by walking.
In time I'll forget this empty brimming,
I may laugh again at
a bird, perhaps, chucking the nest—
but it will not be happiness,
for I have known that.

EXIT

Just when hope withers, a reprieve is granted.
The door opens onto a street like in the movies,
clean of people, of cats; except it is *your* street
you are leaving. Reprieve has been granted,
"provisionally"—a fretful word.

The windows you have closed behind
you are turning pink, doing what they do
every dawn. Here it's gray; the door
to the taxicab waits. This suitcase,
the saddest object in the world.

Well, the world's open. And now through
the windshield the sky begins to blush,
as you did when your mother told you
what it took to be a woman in this life.

AFIELD

Out where crows dip to their kill
under the clouds' languid white oars
she wanders, hands pocketed, hair combed tight
so she won't feel the breeze quickening—
as if she were trying to get back to him,
find the breach in the green
that would let her slip through,
then tug meadow over the wound like a sheet.

I've walked there, too: he can't give
you up, so you give in until you can't live
without him. Like these blossoms, white sores
burst upon earth's ignorant flesh, at first sight
everything is innocence—
then it's itch, scratch, putrescence.

LOST BRILLIANCE

I miss that corridor drenched in shadow,
sweat of centuries steeped into stone.
After the plunge, after my shrieks
diminished and his oars sighed
up to the smoking shore,
the bulwark's gray pallor soothed me.
Even the columns seemed kind, their murky sheen
like the lustrous skin of a roving eye.

I used to stand at the top of the stair
where the carpet flung down
its extravagant heart. Flames
teased the lake into glimmering licks.
I could pretend to be above the earth
rather than underground: a Venetian
palazzo or misty chalet tucked into
an Alp, that mixture of comfort
and gloom . . . nothing was simpler

to imagine. But it was more difficult
each evening to descend: all that marble
flayed with the red plush of privilege
I traveled on, slow nautilus
unwinding in terrified splendor
to where he knew to meet me—
my consort, my match,
though much older and sadder.

In time, I lost the capacity
for resolve. It was as if
I had been traveling all these years
without a body,
until his hands found me—
and then there was just
the two of us forever:
one who wounded,
and one who served.

VI

Now, for the first time, the god lifts his hand,
the fragments join in me with their own music.

—MURIEL RUKEYSER,
"The Poem as Mask"

POLITICAL
(for Breyten Breytenbach)

There was a man spent seven years in hell's circles—
no moon or starlight, shadows singing
their way to slaughter. We give him honorary status.
There's a way to study freedom but few have found
it; you must talk yourself to death and then beyond,
destroy time, then refashion it. Even Demeter keeps digging
towards that darkest miracle,
the hope of finding her child unmolested.

This man did something ill advised, for good reason.
(I mean he went about it wrong.)
And paid in shit, the world is shit and shit
can make us grown. It is becoming the season
she was taken from us. Our wail starts up
of its own accord, is mistaken for song.

DEMETER, WAITING

No. Who can bear it. Only someone
who hates herself, who believes
to pull a hand back from a daughter's cheek
is to put love into her pocket—
like one of those ashen Christian
philosophers, or a war-bound soldier.

She is gone again and I will not bear
it, I will drag my grief through a winter
of my own making and refuse
any meadow that recycles itself into
hope. Shit on the cicadas, dry meteor
flash, finicky butterflies! I will wail and thrash
until the whole goddamned golden panorama freezes
over. Then I will sit down to wait for her. Yes.

LAMENTATIONS

Throw open the shutters
to your darkened residences:
can you hear the pipes playing,
their hunger shaking the olive branches?
To hear them sighing and not answer
is to deny this world, descend rung
by rung into no loss and no desire.
Listen: empty yet full, silken
air and brute tongue,
they are saying:
To refuse to be born is one thing—
but once you are here,
you'd do well to stop crying
and suck the good milk in.

TEOTIHUACÁN

The Indian guide explains to the group of poets
how the Aztec slaves found parasites in cocoons
spun like snowdrifts around the spinules
of a cactus pad (his aide scrapes some free with a stick)
and ground them to a fine red paste.
Next, an unassuming stalk which, chewed,
produced a showy green (a younger stalk
made yellow) and these they used
to decorate the Temple of the Sun.
Plumed serpent who reared his head in the east,
his watery body everywhere: Quetzalcoatl
was a white man, blond hair and tall.
It took millions of these bugs to stain a single wall.
The poets scribble in assorted notebooks. The guide moves on.

HISTORY

Everything's a metaphor, some wise
guy said, and his woman nodded, wisely.
Why was this such a discovery
to him? Why did history
happen only on the outside?
She'd watched an embryo track an arc
across her swollen belly from the inside
and knew she'd best
think *knee,* not *tumor* or *burrowing mole,* lest
it emerge a monster. Each craving marks
the soul: splashed white upon a temple the dish
of ice cream, coveted, broken in a wink,
or the pickle duplicated just behind the ear. *Every wish
will find its symbol,* the woman thinks.

USED

The conspiracy's to make us thin. Size threes
are all the rage, and skirts ballooning above twinkling knees
are every man-child's preadolescent dream.
Tabula rasa. No slate's *that* clean—

we've earned the navels sunk in grief
when the last child emptied us of their brief
interior light. Our muscles say *We have been used.*

Have you ever tried silk sheets? I did,
persuaded by postnatal dread
and a Macy's clerk to bargain for more zip.
We couldn't hang on, slipped
to the floor and by morning the quilts
had slid off, too. Enough of guilt—
It's hard work staying cool.

RUSKS

This is how it happened.

Spring wore on my nerves—
all that wheezing and dripping
while others in galoshes
reaped compost and seemed
enamored most of the time.

Why should I be select?

I got tired of tearing myself down.
Let someone else have
the throne of blues for a while,
let someone else suffer mosquitoes.
As my mama always said:
half a happiness is better
than none at goddam all.

MISSING

I am the daughter who went out with the girls,
never checked back in and nothing marked my "last
known whereabouts," not a single glistening petal.

Horror is partial; it keeps you going. A lost
child is a fact hardening around its absence,
a knot in the breast purring *Touch, and I will*

come true. I was "returned," I watched her
watch as I babbled *It could have been worse. . . .*
Who can tell
what penetrates? Pity is the brutal
discipline. Now I understand she can never
die, just as nothing can bring me back—

I am the one who comes and goes;
I am the footfall that hovers.

DEMETER'S PRAYER TO HADES

This alone is what I wish for you: knowledge.
To understand each desire has an edge,
to know we are responsible for the lives
we change. No faith comes without cost,
no one believes without dying.
Now for the first time
I see clearly the trail you planted,
what ground opened to waste,
though you dreamed a wealth
of flowers.

          There are no curses—only mirrors
held up to the souls of gods and mortals.
And so I give up this fate, too.
Believe in yourself,
go ahead—see where it gets you.

VII

Is this the Region, this the Soil, the Clime
Said then the lost Arch Angel, this the seat
That we must change for Heav'n, this mournful glow
For that celestial light?

—JOHN MILTON, *Paradise Lost*

HER ISLAND

the heat, the stench of things,
the unutterable boredom of it all . . .
—H.D., *Notes on Thought and Vision*

Around us: blazed stones, closed ground.
Waiters lounge, stricken with sirocco,
ice cream disintegrates to a sticky residue
fit for flies and ants. Summer, the dead season.
All the temples of Agrigento
line up like a widow's extracted wisdom teeth:
ocher-stained, proud remnants
of the last sturdy thing about her.

We wander among orange peels and wax
wrappings flecked with grease,
tilt our guidebook, pages blank from sun, and peer
up into the bottomless air. Between columns,
blue slashes of a torched heaven. No,
let it go: nothing will come of this.

᾽

Let it go: nothing will come of this
textbook rampaging, though we have found, by
stint and intuition, the chthonic grotto,
closed for the season behind a chicken-wire gate.
We're too well trained to trespass. Clearly
we can imagine what's beyond it. Clearly
we've sought succor in the wrong corner.
Nothing melts faster than resolve in this climate;
we turn to a funny man in our path, old
as everything here is either old
or scathingly young with whippet thighs
clamped over a souped-up Vespa. *You wish*
to visit historic site? We nod, politely;
he shuffles off to find the key.

～

He shuffles off to find the key,
dust blooming between us to obscure
what we had missed on the way in:
at the head of the path a shack
the size of an outhouse from which he now emerges
hobbling, Quasimodo in a sunnier vein.

An eternity at the rusted lock, then down. It's noon:
we must be madder than the English
with their dogs. Look at his shoes,
he's trod them into slippers!
His touch trembles at my arm;
hasn't he seen an American Black
before? We find a common language: German.

～

Before we find a common language—German,
laced with tenth-grade Spanish and
residual Latin—we descend
in silence through the parched orchard.
The way he stops to smile at me
and pat my arm, I'm surely his first
Queen of Sheba.

          The grotto is
a disappointment, as every site has been
so far. Isn't there a way to tip him early
and get the hell back to the car?
Insulting an old man just isn't done.
Nothing to do but help him conjugate
his verbs and smile until our cheeks ache,
our hands admiring every grimy stone.

～

Our hands admiring every grimy stone,
we let our minds drift far afield:
there's a miracle, a lone bird
singing. What's that
he's saying? *Krieg*? Stilted
German, gathered word by word
half a century ago. I shudder

as he motions my husband close, man to man:
would he like to see a true wonder?
No, not dirty. Another temple, overgrown,
lost to busy people—he mimics Fiats
zipping by—a man's shrine, the god
of fire. Ah, Vulcan? Emphatic nod.
He's had the key for many years, they've all forgotten.

～

He's had the key for many years; they've all forgotten
the ugly god, god of all that's modern.
We toil cross-town, down ever-dwindling streets
until we're certain we're about to turn into
the latest victims of a tourist scam. A sharp curve
under the *autostrada* confirms the destiny
we at least should meet head on: we climb
straight through the city dump,
through rotten fruit and Tampax tubes
so our treacherous guide can deliver us into

what couldn't be: a patch of weeds sprouting six—no, seven—
columns, their Doric reserve softened by weather
to tawny indifference. Roosters cluck among the ruins;
traffic whizzes by in heaven.

～

Traffic whizzes by in heaven
for the Sicilians, of that we're certain;
why else are they practicing on earth, hell-bent
to overtake creampuff foreigners in their rented
Chrysler? Ha! Can't they guess a German
plies the wheel? We dash along beside
them, counterclockwise around the island,
not looking for the ironies we see in spades—
Palermo's golden virgin carried down to sea
as a car bomb blows a judge to smoke,
five brides whose lacquered faces echo those
ones staring, self-mocking, from lurid frescoes
at the Villa Casale: *an eye for an eye.* And
everywhere temples, or pieces of them.

～

Everywhere temples, or pieces of them,
lay scattered across the countryside.
These monstrous broken sticks, flung
aside in a celestial bout of I Ching, have become
Sicily's most exalted litter. (The lesser kind
flies out the windows of honking automobiles.)

We circle the island, trailing the sun
on his daily rounds, turning time back
to one infernal story: a girl
pulled into a lake, one perfect oval
hemmed all around by reeds
at the center of the physical world.
We turn inland as if turning a page in a novel:
dry splash of the cicada, no breath from the sea.

～

Dry splash of the cicada, no breath from the sea.
Our maps have not failed us: this is it,

the only body of water for twenty miles,
water black and still as the breath
it harbored; and around this perfect ellipse
they've built . . . a racetrack.

Bleachers. Pit stops. A ten-foot fence
plastered with ads—Castrol, Campari—
and looped barbed wire; no way to get near.
We drive the circumference
with binoculars: no cave, no reeds.
We drive it twice, first one way, then back,
to cancel our rage at the human need
to make a sport of death.

　　　～

To make a sport of death
it must be endless: round and round
till you feel everything you've trained for—
precision, speed, endurance—reduced to this
godawful roar, this vale of sound.

Your head's a furnace: you don't feel it.
Your eyes, two slits in a computer unit.
A vital rule: if two vehicles ahead of you
crash, drive straight toward the fire
and they will have veered away before you get
there. Bell lap, don't look to see who's
gaining. Aim for the tape, aim *through* it.
Then rip the helmet off and poke your head
through sunlight, into flowers.

　　　～

Through sunlight into flowers
she walked, and was pulled down.
A simple story, a mother's deepest
dread—that her child could drown
in sweetness.

Where the chariot went under
no one can fathom. Water keeps its horrors
while Sky proclaims his, hangs them
in stars. Only Earth—wild
mother we can never leave (even now
we've leaned against her, heads bowed
against the heat)—knows
no story's ever finished; it just goes
on, unnoticed in the dark that's all
around us: blazed stones, the ground closed.

ON THE BUS WITH ROSA PARKS

(1999)

CAMEOS

CAMEOS

July 1925

Lucille among the flamingos
is pregnant; is pained
because she cannot stoop to pluck
the plumpest green tomato
deep on the crusted vine.
Lucille considers
the flamingos, guarding in plastic cheer
the birdbath, parched
and therefore
deserted. In her womb
a dull—no, a husky ache.

If she picks it, Joe will come home
for breakfast tomorrow.
She will slice and dip it
in egg and cornmeal and fry
the tart and poison out.
Sobered by the aroma, he'll show
for sure, and sit down
without a mumbling word.
Inconsiderate, then,

the vine that languishes
so!, and the bath sighing for water
while the diffident flamingos arrange
their torchsong tutus.
She alone
is the blues. Pain drives her blank.
Lucille thinks: *I can't*
even see my own feet.

Lucille lies down
between tomatoes
and the pole beans: heavenly shade.
From here everything looks
reptilian. The tomato plops

in her outstretched palm. *Now*
he'll come, she thinks,
and it will be a son.
The birdbath hushes
behind a cloud
of canebreak and blossoming flame.

Night

Joe ain't studying *nobody*.
He laughs his own sweet bourbon banner,
he makes it to work on time.
Late night, Joe retreats through
the straw-link-and-bauble curtain
and up to bed. Joe sleeps. Snores
gently as a child after a day of marbles.

Joe
knows somewhere
he had a father
who would have told him
how to act. Mama,
stout as a yellow turnip,
loved to bewail her wild good luck:
Blackfoot Injun, tall with
hair like a whip. Now

to do it
without him
is the problem. To walk into a day
and quietly absorb.
Joe takes after Mama.
Joe's Mr. Magoo.
Joe
thinks, half
dreaming, if he ever finds
a place where he can think,
he'd stop clowning
and drinking and then that wife

of his would quit
sending prayers through the chimney.

Ah,
Lucille.
Those eyes, bright and bitter
as cherry bark, those
coltish shins, those thunderous hips!
No wonder he couldn't leave
her be, no wonder whenever she began to show
he packed a fifth and split.

Joe
in funk and sorrow. Joe
in parkbench celibacy, in apostolic
factory rote, in guilt (the brief
astonishment of memory), in grief when
guilt turns monotonous.

He always knows when to go on home.

Birth

(So there you are at last—
a pip, a button in the grass.
The world's begun
without you.

And no reception but
accumulated time.
Your face hidden but your name
shuddering on air!)

Lake Erie Skyline, 1930

He lunges, waits, then strikes again.
I'll make them sweat, he thinks
and does a spider dance
as the fireflies shamble past.

The sky dims slowly; the sun
prefers to do its setting
on the other side of town.
This deeper blue smells
soft. The patterns in it
rearrange—he cups

another fly. (He likes to
shake them dizzy
in his hands, like dice, then
throw them out for luck.
They blink on helplessly
then stagger from the sidewalk
up and gone.)

Sometimes the night arrives
with liquor on its breath,
twice-rinsed and chemical.
Or hopped up, sparking
a nervous shimmy. Or
dangerously still, like his mother
standing next to the stove,
a Bible verse rousing her pursed lips.

He knows what gin is made from—
berries blue. He knows
that Jesus Saves. (His father
calls it Bitches' Tea.)

And sisters—so many, their
names fantastic, myriad
as the points of a chandelier:
Corinna, Violet, Mary, Fay,
Suzanna, Kit, and Pearl. Each evening
when they came to check
his bed, he held his breath, and still
he smelled the camphor
and hair pomade. Saw
foreheads sleek, spitcurl
embellishing a cheek, lips

soft and lashes spiked
with vaseline. He waited
to be blessed.
          They were
Holy Vessels, Mother said:
each had to wait
her Turn. And he, somehow,
was part of the waiting, he was
the chain. He was, somehow,
his father.

The latest victim won't
get up—just lies there
in the middle of the walk
illuminating the earth
regular as breath.
He stomps and grinds
his anger in. Pulls
his foot away and yellow
streaks beneath the sole—
eggyolk flame, lurid
smear of sin.

          Sisters,
laughing, take his shoes away
and bring them scraped
and ordinary
back. *Idiots,*
he thinks. *No wonder
there's so many of them.*

But he can't sleep.
All night beneath his bed,
the sun is out.

Depression Years

                              Pearl
                    can't stop eating;
                    she wants to live!

Those professors
have it all backwards:
after fat came merriment,
simply because she was afraid to
face the world, its lukewarm
nonchalance
that generationwise had set
her people in a stupor of
religion and
gambling debts. (Sure, her
mother was an angel
but her daddy was
her man.)

Pearl laughs
a wet red laugh.
Pearl oozes
everywhere. When she was
young, she licked the walls free of chalk; she
ate dust for the minerals.
Now she just
enjoys, and excess
hardens on her like
a shell.
She sheens.

But oh, what
tiny feet! She tipples
down the stairs. She cracks a chair.
The largest baby shoe
is neat. Pearl laughs
when Papa jokes: *Why don't
you grow yourself some feet?*
Her mother calls them
devil's hooves.
Her brother
doesn't
care.
He has
A Brain; he doesn't notice.
She gives him of her own

ham hock, plies him with
sweetened yams. Unravels
ratted sweaters, reworks them
into socks. In the lean years
lines his shoes
with newspaper. *(Main
thing is, you don't
miss school.)*

She tells him
it's the latest style.
He never laughs.
He reads. He
shuts her out.
Pearl thinks
she'll never marry—
though she'd
like to have
a child.

Homework

"The Negro and his song
are inseparable.
If his music is primitive
and if it has much that
is sensuous, this is simply
a part of giving
pleasure, a quality
appealing strongly
to the Negro's
entire being. Indeed,
his love of rhythms
and melody, his
childish faith
in dreams . . ."
Shit,
he'll take Science, most
Exacting Art.
In school when the teacher

makes him lead
the class in song,
he'll cough straight through.
Better
columns of figures, the thing
dissected to the bone.
Better
the clear and incurious *drip*
of fluid from pipet
to reassuring beaker.
     "The Negro claps his hands
     spontaneously; his feet
     move constantly in joyful
     anticipation of the drum. . . ."
Most of all
he'd like to study
the composition of the stars.

Graduation, Grammar School

Joe
holds both
fists out, palms
down. *Come on boy, guess.*

The boy
hesitates. He knows
there's nothing
in either one.
    (The game:
    Who offers the hand
    first, man or woman?
    Who first lowers
    the eyes? If the hand
    is not received, whose
    price is reduced? And
    what if both are men?
    Or drunk? Or one is
    white? The possibilities
    are infinite.)

Joe
sees his son
flicker. Although
the air is not a glass,
watches as he puts his lips to
the brim—then turns away, bored.
He is not mine, this son
who ripens, quiet
poison on a
shelf.

Painting the Town

The mirror
in the hall is red.
Pearl
giggles: *Pretty*
as a freshly painted
barn. She tugs
a wrinkle down.
Since she's discovered
men would rather drown
than nibble,
she does just
fine.

She'd like to show
her brother
what it is like to crawl
up the curved walls
of the earth, or
to be that earth—but
he has other plans.
Which is alright. Which is
As It Should Be.
Let the boy reach manhood
anyway he can.

Easter Sunday, 1940

A purity
in sacrifice, a blessedness
in shame. Lucille
in full regalia, clustered
violets and crucifix.
She shoos
a hornet
back to Purgatory,
rounds the corner, finds
her son in shirtsleeves staring
from the porch into the yard
as if it were the sea.

And suddenly
she doesn't care.
(Joe, after all, came home.)
She feels as if
she's on her back
again, and all around her
blushing thicket.

Nightwatch. The Son.

(Aggressively adult,
they keep their
lives, to which
I am a witness.

At the other end
I orbit, pinpricked
light. I watch.
I float and grieve.)

FREEDOM: BIRD'S-EYE VIEW

SINGSONG

When I was young, the moon spoke in riddles
and the stars rhymed. I was a new toy
waiting for my owner to pick me up.

When I was young, I ran the day to its knees.
There were trees to swing on, crickets for capture.

I was narrowly sweet, infinitely cruel,
tongued in honey and coddled in milk,
sunburned and silvery and scabbed like a colt.

And the world was already old.
And I was older than I am today.

I CUT MY FINGER ONCE ON PURPOSE

I'm no baby. There's no grizzly man
wheezing in the back of the closet.
When I was the only one,
they asked me if I wanted a night-light
and I said *yes*—
but then came the shadows.

I know they make the noises at night.

My toy monkey Giselle, I put her
in a red dress they said was mine
once—but if it was mine, why did they yell
when Giselle clambered up the porch maple
and tore it? Why would Mother say
When you grow up, I hope you have
a daughter just like you

if it weren't true, that I *have* a daughter
hidden in the closet—someone
they were ashamed of and locked away
when I was too small to cry?

I watch them all the time now:
Mother burned herself at the stove
without wincing. Father
smashed a thumb in the Ford,
then stuck it in his mouth for show.
They bought my brother a just-for-boys
train, so I grabbed the caboose
and crowned him—but he toppled
from his rocker without a bleat;
he didn't even bleed.

That's when I knew they were
robots. But I'm no idiot:
I eat everything they give me,
I let them put my monkey away.
When I'm big enough
I'll go in, past the boa
and the ginger fox biting its tail
to where my girl lies, waiting . . .
and we'll stay there, quiet,
until daylight finds us.

PARLOR

We passed through
on the way to anywhere else.
No one lived there
but silence, a pale china gleam,

and the tired eyes of saints
aglow on velvet.

Mom says things are made
to be used. But Grandma insisted
peace was in what wasn't there,
strength in what was unsaid.

It would be nice to have a room
you couldn't enter, except in your mind.
I like to sit on my bed
plugged into my transistor radio,
"Moon River" pouring through my head.

How do you *use* life?
How do you *feel* it? Mom says

things harden with age; she says
Grandma is happier now. After the funeral,
I slipped off while they stood around
remembering—away from all
the talking and eating and weeping

to sneak a peek. She wasn't there.
Then I understood why
she had kept them just so:

so quiet and distant,
the things that she loved.

THE FIRST BOOK

Open it.

Go ahead, it won't bite.
Well . . . maybe a little.

More a nip, like. A tingle.
It's pleasurable, really.

You see, it keeps on opening.
You may fall in.

Sure, it's hard to get started;
remember learning to use

knife and fork? Dig in:
You'll never reach bottom.

It's not like it's the end of the world—
just the world as you think

you know it.

MAPLE VALLEY BRANCH LIBRARY, 1967

For a fifteen-year-old there was plenty
to do: Browse the magazines,
slip into the Adult Section to see
what vast *tristesse* was born of rush-hour traffic,
décolletés, and the plague of too much money.
There was so much to discover—how to
lay out a road, the language of flowers,
and the place of women in the tribe of Moost.
There were equations elegant as a French twist,
fractal geometry's unwinding maple leaf;

I could follow, step-by-step, the slow disclosure
of a pineapple Jell-O mold—or take
the path of Harold's purple crayon through
the bedroom window and onto a lavender
spill of stars. Oh, I could walk any aisle
and smell wisdom, put a hand out to touch
the rough curve of bound leather,
the harsh parchment of dreams.

As for the improbable librarian
with her salt and paprika upsweep,
her British accent and sweater clip
(mom of a kid I knew from school)—
I'd go up to her desk and ask for help
on bareback rodeo or binary codes,
phonics, Gestalt theory,
lead poisoning in the Late Roman Empire,

the play of light in Dutch Renaissance painting;
I would claim to be researching
pre-Columbian pottery or Chinese foot-binding,
but all I wanted to know was:
Tell me what you've read that keeps
that half smile afloat
above the collar of your impeccable blouse.

So I read *Gone with the Wind* because
it was big, and haiku because they were small.
I studied history for its rhapsody of dates,
lingered over Cubist art for the way
it showed all sides of a guitar at once.
All the time in the world was there, and sometimes
all the world on a single page.
As much as I could hold
on my plastic card's imprint I took,

greedily: six books, six volumes of bliss,
the stuff we humans are made of:
words and sighs and silence,
ink and whips, Brahma and cosine,
corsets and poetry and blood sugar levels—
I carried it home, past five blocks of aluminum siding
and the old garage where, on its boarded-up doors,
someone had scrawled:

I CAN EAT AN ELEPHANT
IF I TAKE SMALL BITES.

Yes, I said, to no one in particular: *That's*
what I'm gonna do!

FREEDOM: BIRD'S-EYE VIEW

The sun flies over the madrigals,
outsmarting the magisterial
wits, sad ducks

who imagine they matter.
What a parade! Wind tucks
a Dixie cup up its
sleeve, absconds
with a kid's bright chatter
while above, hawks
wheel as the magistrates circle
below, clutching their hats.

I'm not buying. To watch
the tops of 10,000
heads floating by on sticks
and not care if one of them
sees me (though it
would be a kick!)
—now, that's
what I'd call
freedom,
and justice,
and ice cream for all.

TESTIMONIAL

Back when the earth was new
and heaven just a whisper,
back when the names of things
hadn't had time to stick;

back when the smallest breezes
melted summer into autumn,
when all the poplars quivered
sweetly in rank and file . . .

the world called, and I answered.
Each glance ignited to a gaze.
I caught my breath and called that life,
swooned between spoonfuls of lemon sorbet.

I was pirouette and flourish,
I was filigree and flame.
How could I count my blessings
when I didn't know their names?

Back when everything was still to come,
luck leaked out everywhere.
I gave my promise to the world,
and the world followed me here.

DAWN REVISITED

Imagine you wake up
with a second chance: The blue jay
hawks his pretty wares
and the oak still stands, spreading
glorious shade. If you don't look back,

the future never happens.
How good to rise in sunlight,
in the prodigal smell of biscuits—
eggs and sausage on the grill.
The whole sky is yours

to write on, blown open
to a blank page. Come on,
shake a leg! You'll never know
who's down there, frying those eggs,
if you don't get up and see.

BLACK ON A
SATURDAY NIGHT

MY MOTHER ENTERS THE WORK FORCE

The path to ABC Business School
was paid for by a lucky sign:
ALTERATIONS, QUALIFIED SEAMSTRESS INQUIRE WITHIN.
Tested on sleeves, hers
never puckered—puffed or sleek,
leg-o'-mutton or raglan—
they barely needed the damp cloth
to steam them perfect.

Those were the afternoons. Evenings
she took in piecework, the treadle machine
with its locomotive whir
traveling the lit path of the needle
through quicksand taffeta
or velvet deep as a forest.
And now and now sang the treadle,
I know, I know. . . .

And then it was day again, all morning
at the office machines, their clack and chatter
another journey—rougher,
that would go on forever
until she could break a hundred words
with no errors—ah, and then

no more postponed groceries,
and that blue pair of shoes!

BLACK ON A SATURDAY NIGHT

This is no place for lilac
or somebody on a trip
to themselves. Hips
are an asset here, and color
calculated to flash
lemon bronze cerise

in the course of a dip and turn.
Beauty's been caught lying
and the truth's rubbed raw:
Here, you get your remorse
as a constitutional right.

It's always what we don't
fear that happens, always
not now and why are
you people acting this way
(meaning we put in petunias
instead of hydrangeas and reject
ecru as a fashion statement).

But we can't do it—naw, because
the wages of living are sin
and the wages of sin are love
and the wages of love are pain
and the wages of pain are philosophy
and that leads definitely to an attitude
and an attitude will get you
nowhere fast so you might as well
keep dancing dancing till
tomorrow gives up with a shout,
'cause there is only
Saturday night, and we are in it—
black as black can,
black as black does,
not a concept
nor a percentage
but a natural law.

THE MUSICIAN TALKS ABOUT "PROCESS"
(after Anthony "Spoons" Pough)

I learned the spoons from
my grandfather, who was blind.
Every day he'd go into the woods

'cause that was his thing.
He met all kinds of creatures,
birds and squirrels,
and while he was feeding them
he'd play the spoons,
and after they finished
they'd stay and listen.

When I go into Philly
on a Saturday night,
I don't need nothing but
my spoons and the music.
Laid out on my knees
they look so quiet,
but when I pick them up
I can play to anything:
a dripping faucet,
a tambourine,
fish shining in a creek.

A funny thing:
When my grandfather died,
every creature sang.
And when the men went out
to get him, they kept singing.
They sung for two days,
all the birds, all the animals.
That's when I left the South.

SUNDAY

Their father was a hunting man.
Each spring the Easter rabbit sprung open
above the bathroom sink, drip slowed
by the split pink pods of its ears
to an intravenous trickle.
There was the occasional deer,
though he had no particular taste

for venison—too stringy, he said,
but made Mother smoke it up just in case,
all four haunches and the ribs.

Summer always ended with a catfish,
large as a grown man's thigh
severed at the hip, thrashing
in a tin washtub: a mean fish, a fish
who knew the world was to be endured
between mud and the shining hook.

He avoided easy quarry: possum
and squirrel, complacent carp.
He wouldn't be caught dead
bagging coon; coon, he said,
was fickle meat—tasted like
chicken one night, the next like
poor man's lobster. He'd never admit
being reduced to eating coon,
to be called out of his name
and into that cartoon.

It's not surprising they could eat the mess
he made of their playground: They watched
the October hog gutted with grim fury,
a kind of love gone wrong, but oh
they adored each whiskery hock, each
ham slice brushed subterranean green.

They were eating his misery
like bad medicine meant to help them
grow. They would have done anything
not to see his hand jerk like that,
his belt hissing through the loops and around
that fist working inside the coils
like an animal gnawing, an animal
who knows freedom's worth anything
you need to leave behind to get to it—
even your own flesh and blood.

THE CAMEL COMES TO US
FROM THE BARBARIANS

This one is enormous: rough-cut,
the fur like matted felt—
and so much of it,

rising in vulgar mounds upon its back
as if the sand itself had belched
into heaven's beard. Gods,

what malevolence! The eye a constant
rolling orb, glistening with ill intent,
yellowed, gummed with hair, more hairs

than you or I would care to count,
that eye marks every move its jailer makes
and waits for him to step too near—

one blow would cripple any man.
Another specimen stands bellowing
beneath the farthest palm. Though slighter,

it daunts equally, staked haunches
straining, muscles potent as the reek
that saturates our sun-baked marketplace.

About the larger one some purpose lurks:
Hindquarters splayed, it tugs against its ropes,
snorts, yearns its massive head and slavers

toward that godawful sound. Could
the drabber one be female, and its mate?
More monsters in our midst!

And yet . . . if these vile creatures be
like geese, or dogs, and their offspring
learn to cuddle the one

who coddles them first—why,
our fortune's pegged for sure.
Let us display our sternest countenance,

then apportion what they most desire
according to the measure of their service.
A rare commodity, these beasts—

who cannot know
what beauty wreaks, what mountains
pity moves.

THE VENUS OF WILLENDORF

Let your eye be a candle in a chamber,
your gaze a wick;
let me be blind enough
to ignite it.
                    —PAUL CELAN

She kneels on a workbench
strewn with clipper and trowel
to look out over the valley, red sun
still snagged on the farthest green fringe.
She's early. Behind her
scratch the arbor's last leaves
and a few gray birds pecking for crumbs
among the rose husks fallen to the veranda.

Arrived a week ago, one more exotic
in the stream of foreign students
invited to *Herr Professor*'s summer house
in the Wachau, she was taken
straight from train to tavern
to see the village miracle, unearthed
not five kilometers from this garden shed:

the legendary Venus of Willendorf.
Just a replica, *natürlich,*

a handful of primitive stone
entombed in a glass display
the innkeeper kept dusting as he told
his one story, charmed by the sight of
a live black girl. *Not five kilometers!*
he repeated, stopping his cloth
to reexamine the evidence:
sprawling buttocks and barbarous thighs,
breasts heaped up in her arms
to keep from spilling.
We should have kept her, he said.
Made the world come to us
here, in Austria.

                                    "Here" seemed
hardly Austrian, although the Danube
had wandered through, scooped out a gorge
and left it clotted with poppies to dream
the haze of centuries away. Each morning
she heard children tumbling down the path
to catch the 7:10 on its milk run
to the school in Krems. Each evening
the Munich-Vienna express barreled through
at precisely—another miracle—
7:10.

                          It was impossible, of course,
to walk the one asphalted street
without enduring a gauntlet of stares.
Have you seen her? they asked,
comparing her to their Venus
until she could feel her own breasts
settle and the ripening
predicament of hip and thigh.

They were on the veranda
when he confessed—no, "confided"
(wife occupied in the kitchen, slicing cake)
that his pubic hair had gone white.
She should have been shocked

but couldn't deny the thrill
it gave her, how her body felt
tender and fierce, all at once.
What made one sculpture so luscious
when there were real women, layered
in flesh no one worshipped?
The professor's wife, for instance,
hair too long and charred eyes
wild in their sockets as if to say
Where thou goest, there I went also—
no one devoured her with his glance as she
cleared away the tea things.

In Willendorf

twilight is brutal: no dim tottering
across flowery fields but blindness
dropped into the treeline like an ax.
He won't dare touch me,
she argues, *and risk destroying*
everything. Yet his gaze, glutting itself
until her contours blazed . . .
and suddenly she understands what made
the Venus beautiful
was how the carver's hand had loved her,
that visible caress.

Lightning

then a faint, agreeable thunder
as the express glides past below,
passengers snared in light, smudged flecks
floating in a string of golden cells.
If only we were ghosts, she thinks,
leaning into the rising hush,

if only I could wait forever.

INCARNATION IN PHOENIX

Into this paradise of pain she strides
on the slim tether of a nurse's bell,
her charcoal limbs emerging from crisp whites
unlikely as an envelope issuing smoke.
I've rung because my breasts have risen,
artesian: I'm not ready for this motherhood stuff.

Her name is Raven. And she swoops
across the tiled wilderness, hair boiling
thunder over the rampart of bobby pins
spoking her immaculate cap. She dips once
for the baby just waking, fists punching
in for work "right on schedule"—
bends again to investigate what
should be natural, milk sighing into
one tiny, vociferous mouth. "Ah,"
she whispers, "ambrosia,"

shaming me instantly. But
no nectar trickles forth, no manna
descends from the vault of heaven
to feed this pearly syllable, this
package of leafy persuasion
dropped on our doorstep and ripening
before us, a miniature United Nations
"Just like me!" Raven says, citing

the name of her mother's village
somewhere in Norway, her father
a buffalo soldier. Now,
of course, we can place her:
an African Valkyrie
who takes my breast in her fists
grunting, "This hurts you more
than it does me"—then my laugh
squeezed to a whimper and the milk running out.

REVENANT

BEST WESTERN MOTOR LODGE,
   AAA APPROVED

Where can I find Moon Avenue,
just off Princess Lane? I wandered
the length of the Boulevard of the Spirits,
squandered a wad on Copper Queen Drive;

stood for a while at the public drinking fountain,
where a dog curled into his own hair
and a boy knelt, cursing his dirtied
tennis shoes. I tell you, if you feel strange,

strange things will happen to you:
Fallen peacocks on the library shelves
and all those maple trees, plastering
the sidewalks with leaves,

bloody palm prints everywhere.

REVENANT

Palomino, horse of shadows.
Pale of the gyrfalcon
streaking free,
a reckoning—

the dark climbing out a crack in the earth.

Black veils starched for Easter.
The black hood of the condemned,
reeking with slobber.
The no color behind the eyelid
as the ax drops.

Gauze bandages over the wounds of State.

The canvas is primed, the morning
bitten off but too much to chew.
No angels here:
The last one slipped the room
while your head was turned,

made off for the winter streets.

ON VERONICA

*"I sat in front of the mirror, covered it over with
plastic and copied on it the outlines of my face."*
—EWA KURYLUK, *Journey to the Frontiers of Art*

Exposed to light,
the shroud lifts
its miraculous inscription—

a wound. Skin talking:
yes there, touch me there.
The stain of a glance,

a glance caught off-
guard, how it slices,
how each mirror imperils!

Or the acid sweat of sex,
cool ache of a breeze . . .
a hassock, stars.

Heaven encoded in the blue
volume of an arch
imploding,

shadows burned into doorways
at the zero point.
Dots and dashes.

The beloved's face
captured, rising from zero
onto the glistening plate—

white room, white sky.

THERE CAME A SOUL

After IVAN ALBRIGHT'S *Into the World There Came a Soul Called Ida*

She arrived as near to virginal
as girls got in those days—i.e., young,
the requisite dewy cheek
flushed at its own daring.
He had hoped for a little more edge.
But she held the newspaper rolled like a scepter,
his advertisement turned up to prove
she was there solely at his bidding—and yet
the gold band, the photographs . . . a mother, then.

He placed her in the old garden chair,
the same one he went to evenings
when the first tug on the cord sent the bulb
swinging like the lamps in the medic's tent
over the wounded, swaddled shapes that moaned
each time the Screaming Meemies let loose,
their calculated shrieks so far away
he thought of crickets—while all around him
matted gauze and ether pricked up
an itch so bad he could hardly sketch
each clean curve of tissue opening.
I shut my eyes, walk straight to it.
Nothing special but it's there, wicker
fraying under my calming fingers.

What if he changed the newspaper into a letter,
then ripped it up and tucked the best part
from view? How much he needed that desecrated
scrap! And the red comb snarled with a few

317

pale hairs for God in his infinite greed
to snatch upon like a hawk targeting a sparrow—
he couldn't say *At least I let you keep your hair*
so he kept to his task, applying paint
like a bandage to the open wound.

Pretty Ida, out to earn a penny
for her tiny brood.
He didn't mask the full lips
or the way all the niggling fears
of an adolescent century
shone through her hesitant eyes,
but he painted the room out, blackened
every casement, every canvas drying
along the wall, even the ailing coffeepot
whose dim brew she politely refused,
until she was seated
as he had been, dropped
bleak and thick,
onto the last chair in the world.

THE PEACH ORCHARD

What the soul needs, it uses.
—JAMES HILLMAN

I say there is no memory of him
staining my palms and my mouth.
I walk about, no longer human—
something shameful, something
that can't move at all.

Women invented misery,
but we don't understand it.
We hold it close and tell it
everything, cradle the ache
until it seeps in and he's

gone, just like the wind
when the air stands still.
I'll step lightly
along the path between
the blossoming trees,

lightly over petals
drifting speechless and pale.
No other story could have
brought me here: this
stone floor. And branches,

bank upon bank of them brimming
like a righteous mob, like
a ventriloquist humming,
his hand up
my spine . . . O these

trees, shedding all
over themselves.
Only a fool
would think such frenzy
beautiful.

AGAINST REPOSE

(Balcony, Berlin, 1981)

Nothing comes to mind.

I place my arm on my knee
and a small ache shimmers
in the elbow. Gristle
perhaps, or the nub of a nerve.
Who knows? Don't think;
lean into the wrought iron
until the table quakes, sends the wine aquiver.

Nothing happens.
Red homunculus settling,
green—*Libelle*? cicada?—drifting by
as a breeze rouses the linden,
lifts a millimeter of leaf
all the way down the boulevard.
This elbow's no good. I'd rather be

anywhere—and if I dare blink
or belch, or scratch at my furrowed unease;
if I refuse to look up, into God's
bland countenance . . .
the lost wing would still itch
and the wine stay bitter
in the glass—a mouthful of sin

in an inchful of hell.

AGAINST SELF-PITY

It gets you nowhere but deeper into
your own shit—pure misery a luxury
one never learns to enjoy. There's always some

meatier malaise, a misalliance ripe
to burst: Soften the mouth to a smile and
it stutters; laugh, and your drink spills onto the wake

of repartee gone cold. Oh, you know
all the right things to say to yourself: Seize
the day, keep the faith, remember the children

starving in India . . . the same stuff
you say to your daughter
whenever a poked-out lip betrays

a less than noble constitution. (Not that
you'd consider actually *going* to India—all
those diseases and fervent eyes.) But if it's

not your collapsing line of credit, it's
the scream you let rip when a centipede
shrieks up the patio wall. And that

daughter? She'll find a reason to laugh
at you, her dear mother: *Poor thing
wouldn't harm a soul!* she'll say, as if

she knew of such things—
innocence, and a soul smart enough to know
when to get out of the way.

GÖTTERDÄMMERUNG

A straw reed climbs the car antenna.

Beyond the tinted glass, golden waves
of grain. *Golly!* I can't help
exclaiming, and he smirks—
my born-again naturalist son
with his souped-up laptop,
dear prodigy who insists
on driving the two hours
to the jet he insists I take.
(No turboprops for this

old lady.) On good days
I feel a little meaty; on bad,
a few degrees from rancid.
(Damn knee: I used it this morning
to retrieve a spilled colander;
now every cell's blowing whistles.)

At least it's still a body.
He'd never believe it, son of mine,
but I remember what it's like
to walk the world
with no help from strangers,

not even a personal trainer
to make you feel the burn.

(Most of the time, it's flutter-heart
and Her Royal Celestial Mustache.
Most of the time I'm broth
instead of honey in the bag.)

So I wear cosmetics maliciously
now. And I like my bracelets,
even though they sound ridiculous,
clinking as I skulk through the mall,
store to store like some ancient
iron-clawed griffin—but I've never

stopped wanting to cross
the equator, or touch an elk's
horns, or sing *Tosca* or screw
James Dean in a field of wheat.
To hell with wisdom. They're all wrong:
I'll never be through with my life.

GHOST WALK

Château de Lavigny
August 1996

The neighbors who never
set foot in the castle
never tasted the truffles or château rosé
say she walks room to room
all night turning the lights on
and by day a cold wind blows
through the tiered gardens
pinching leaves from the withering rose

It is said in the village
she died of pure heartbreak

not a love turned away
but a love lasting only
as long as a lifetime
his life and no longer
not enough for the lady
hair red as a brushfire

that refused to go out
though it faded with years
to the orange of the coral
that lives in the sea
and still she was lovely
pale beauty became her
like pearls or a music box
like *Kaffee mit Schlag*

slim in an era when slim wasn't in fashion
she climbed into her tub
lined with bath salts and mirrors
chin-deep in scent
she would dream of a body
that could hold all of her
keep her afloat on this ocean
of good sense and breeding

she told no one not even
the one man she lived for
she put on her lipstick
she combed her brave hair
which she bore like a lantern
into the murmuring parlor
where they waited with smiles
and champagne on their lips

all night the waves pitching
all day the crows wheeling
through skies blue as his eyes
bright above the stunned lake
when he died she lay down

in their bed of silk tassels
in their bed of fringed curtains
and rose-colored satin

she lay down without tears
in that blushing cradle
and slept in that rocking
that cargo of sighs
each night the bed creaking
cast onto the waves
each dawn roses flaunting
their loose tongues of flame

she's a kind spirit
they assure us
down in the village
poor soul left behind
when the party was over
searching the rooms
for his laughter
and a last glass of wine

LADY FREEDOM AMONG US

don't lower your eyes
or stare straight ahead to where
you think you ought to be going

don't mutter *oh no*
not another one
get a job   fly a kite
go bury a bone

with her oldfashioned sandals
with her leaden skirts
with her stained cheeks and whiskers and heaped up trinkets
she has risen among us in blunt reproach

she has fitted her hair under a hand-me-down cap
and spruced it up with feathers and stars
slung over one shoulder she bears
the rainbowed layers of charity and murmurs
all of you   even the least of you

don't cross to the other side of the square
don't think *another item to fit on a tourist's agenda*

consider her drenched gaze   her shining brow
she who has brought mercy back into the streets
and will not retire politely to the potter's field

having assumed the thick skin of this town
its gritted exhaust its sunscorch and blear
she rests in her weathered plumage
bigboned   resolute

don't think you can ever forget her
don't even try
she's not going to budge

no choice but to grant her space
crown her with sky
for she is one of the many
and she is each of us

FOR SOPHIE, WHO'LL BE
IN FIRST GRADE IN THE YEAR 2000

No bright toy
this world we've left you.
Even the wrapping
is torn, the ribbons
grease-flecked and askew.
Still, it's all we have.

Wait a moment before
you pick it up. Study
its scratches, how it
shines in places. Now
love what you touch,
and you will touch wisely.

May the world, in your hands,
brighten with use. May you
sleep in sweet breath and
rise always in wonder
to mountain and forest,
green gaze and silk cheek—

dear Sophie,
littlest phoenix.

ON THE BUS WITH ROSA PARKS

*All history is a negotiation
between familiarity and
strangeness.*

—SIMON SCHAMA

SIT BACK, RELAX

Lord, Lord. No rest
for the wicked?
Most likely no
heating pads.

*(Heat some gravy for the potatoes,
slice a little green pepper
into the pinto beans . . .)*

Sometimes a body
just plain grieves.

Stand by me in this, my hour—

"THE SITUATION IS INTOLERABLE"

Intolerable: that civilized word.
Aren't we civilized, too? Shoes shined,
each starched cuff unyielding,
each dovegray pleated trouser leg
a righteous sword advancing
onto the field of battle
in the name of the Lord . . .

Hush, now. Assay
the terrain: all around us dark
and the perimeter in flames,
but the stars—
tiny, missionary stars—
on high, serene, studding
the inky brow of heaven.

So what if we were born up a creek
and knocked flat with the paddle,
if we ain't got a pot to piss in
and nowhere to put it if we did?

Our situation is intolerable, but what's worse
is to sit here and do nothing.
O yes. O mercy on our souls.

FREEDOM RIDE

As if, after High Street
and the left turn onto Exchange,
the view would veer onto
someplace fresh: Curaçao,
or a mosque adrift on a milk-fed pond.
But there's just more cloud cover,
and germy air
condensing on the tinted glass,
and the little houses with
their fearful patches of yard
rushing into the flames.

Pull the cord a stop too soon, and
you'll find yourself walking
a gauntlet of stares.
Daydream, and you'll wake up
in the stale dark of a cinema,
Dallas playing its mistake over and over
until even that sad reel won't stay
stuck—there's still
Bobby and Malcolm and Memphis,
at every corner the same
scorched brick, darkened windows.

Make no mistake: There's fire
back where you came from, too.
Pick any stop: You can ride
into the afternoon singing with strangers,
or rush home to the scotch
you've been pouring all day—
but where you sit is where you'll be
when the fire hits.

CLIMBING IN

Teeth.
Metallic. Lie-gapped.
Not a friendly shine

like the dime
cutting my palm
as I clutch the silver pole
to step up, up

(sweat gilding the dear lady's
cheek)—these are big teeth,
teeth of the wolf

under Grandmother's cap.
Not quite a grin.
Pay him to keep smiling

as the bright lady tumbles
head over tail
down the clinking gullet.

CLAUDETTE COLVIN GOES TO WORK

> *Another Negro woman has been arrested and thrown into jail*
> *because she refused to get up out of her seat on the bus and*
> *give it to a white person. This is the second time since the*
> *Claudette Colbert [sic] case. . . . This must be stopped.*
> —BOYCOTT FLIER, December 5, 1955

Menial twilight sweeps the storefronts along Lexington
as the shadows arrive to take their places
among the scourge of the earth. Here and there
a fickle brilliance—lightbulbs coming on
in each narrow residence, the golden wattage
of bleak interiors announcing *Anyone home?*
or *I'm beat, bring me a beer.*

Mostly I say to myself *Still here*. Lay
my keys on the table, pack the perishables away
before flipping the switch. I like the sugary
look of things in bad light—one drop of sweat
is all it would take to dissolve an armchair pillow
into brocade residue. Sometimes I wait until
it's dark enough for my body to disappear;

then I know it's time to start out for work.
Along the Avenue, the cabs start up, heading
toward midtown; neon stutters into ecstasy
as the male integers light up their smokes and let loose
a stream of brave talk: "Hey Mama" souring quickly to
"Your Mama" when there's no answer—as if
the most injury they can do is insult the reason

you're here at all, walking in your whites
down to the stop so you can make a living.
So ugly, so fat, so dumb, so greasy—
What do we have to do to make God love us?
Mama was a maid; my daddy mowed lawns like a boy,
and I'm the crazy girl off the bus, the one
who wrote in class she was going to be President.

I take the Number 6 bus to the Lex Ave train
and then I'm there all night, adjusting the sheets,
emptying the pans. And I don't curse or spit
or kick and scratch like they say I did then.
I help those who can't help themselves,
I do what needs to be done . . . and I sleep
whenever sleep comes down on me.

THE ENACTMENT

"I'm just a girl who people were mean to
on a bus. . . . I could have been anybody."
—MARY WARE, née SMITH

Can't use no teenager, especially
no poor black trash,
no matter what her parents do
to keep up a living. Can't use
anyone without sense enough
to bite their tongue.

It's gotta be a woman,
someone of standing:
preferably shy, preferably married.
And she's got to know
when the moment's right.
Stay polite, though her shoulder's
aching, bus driver
the same one threw her off
twelve years before.

Then all she's got to do is
sit there, quiet, till
the next moment finds her—and only then
can she open her mouth to ask
Why do you push us around?
and his answer: *I don't know but*
the law is the law and you

are under arrest.
She must sit there, and not smile
as they enter to carry her off;
she must know who to call
who will know whom else to call
to bail her out . . . and only then

can she stand up and exhale,
can she walk out the cell
and down the jail steps

into flashbulbs and
her employer's white
arms—and go home,
and sit down in the seat
we have prepared for her.

ROSA

How she sat there,
the time right inside a place
so wrong it was ready.

That trim name with
its dream of a bench
to rest on. Her sensible coat.

Doing nothing was the doing:
the clean flame of her gaze
carved by a camera flash.

How she stood up
when they bent down to retrieve
her purse. That courtesy.

QE2. TRANSATLANTIC CROSSING. THIRD DAY.

Panel of gray silk. Liquefied ashes. Dingy percale tugged over
the vast dim earth—ill-fitting, softened by eons of tossing
and turning, unfurling its excesses, recalling its losses,
no seam for the mending, no selvage to catch and align
from where I sit and look out from this rose-colored armchair
along the gallery. I can hear the chime of the elevator,

the hush of trod carpet. Beyond the alcove, escorted widows
perfect a slow rumba. Couples linger by the cocktail piano,
enmeshed in their own delight as others stroll past,

pause to remark on the weather. Mist, calm seas.
This is a journey for those who simply wish to be
on the way—to lie back and be rocked for a while, dangled

between the silver spoon and golden gate. Even
I'm thrilled, who never learned to wait on a corner,
hunched in bad weather, or how many coins to send
clicking into the glass bowl. I can only imagine
what it's like to climb the steel stairs and sit down, to feel
the weight of yourself sink into the moment of *going home*.

This is not the exalted fluorescence of the midnight route,
exhaustion sweetening the stops. There's
no money here, just chips and signatures,
no neat dime or tarnished token, no exact change.
Here I float on the lap of existence. Each night
I put this body into its sleeve of dark water with no more

than a teardrop of ecstasy, a thimbleful of ache.
And that, friends, is the difference—
I can't erase an ache I never had.
Not even my own grandmother would pity me;
instead she'd suck her teeth at the sorry sight
of some Negro actually looking for misery.

Well. I'd go home if I knew where to get off.

IN THE LOBBY OF THE WARNER THEATRE, WASHINGTON, D.C.

They'd positioned her—two attendants flanking the wheelchair—
at the foot of the golden escalator, just right
of the movie director who had cajoled her to come.
Elegant in a high-strung way, a-twitch in his tux,
he shoved half spectacles up the nonexistent
bridge of his nose. Not that he was using her
to push his film, but it was only right (wasn't it?)
that she be wherever history was being made—after all,

she was the true inspiration, she was *living* history.
The audience descended in a cavalcade of murmuring
sequins. She waited. She knew how to abide,
to sit in cool contemplation of the expected.
She had learned to travel a crowd
bearing a smile we weren't sure we could bear
to receive, it was so calm a suturing.
Scrolling earthward, buffed bronze

in the reflected glow, we couldn't wait but leaned out
to catch a glimpse, and saw
that the smile was not practiced at all—
real delight bloomed there. She was curious;
she suffered our approach (the gush and coo,
the babbling, the director bending down
to meet the camera flash) until someone
tried to touch her, and then the attendants

pushed us back, gently. She nodded,
lifted a hand as if to console us
before letting it drop, slowly, to her lap.
Resting there. The idea of consolation
soothing us: her gesture
already become her touch,
like the history she made for us sitting there,
waiting for the moment to take her.

THE POND, PORCH-VIEW:
SIX P.M., EARLY SPRING

I sit, and sit, and will my thoughts
the way they used to wend
when thoughts were young
(i.e., accused of wandering).
The sunset ticks another notch
into the pressure treated rails
of the veranda. My heart, too,
has come down to earth;

I've missed the chance
to put things in reverse,
recapture childhood's backseat
universe. Where I'm at now
is more like riding on a bus
through unfamiliar neighborhoods—
chair in recline, the view chopped square
and dimming quick. I know
I vowed I'd get off
somewhere grand; like that dear goose
come honking down
from Canada, I tried to end up
anyplace but here.
Who am I kidding? Here I am.

AMERICAN SMOOTH

(2004)

American (ə-mĕr'ĭ-kən) *adj*. 1. Of or relating to the United States of America or its people, language, or culture.

smooth (smoo*th*) *adj*. 1. Having a surface free from irregularities, roughness, or projections: even. . . . 2. Having a fine texture: *a smooth fabric*. . . . 4. Having an even consistency: *a smooth pudding*. 5. Having an even or gentle motion or movement: *a smooth ride*. 6. Having no obstructions or difficulties: *a smooth operation*. 7. Serene: *a smooth temperament*. 8. Bland: *a smooth wine*. 9. Ingratiatingly polite and agreeable. See Synonyms at suave. 10. Having no grossness or coarseness in dress or manner.

American Smooth *n*. A form of ballroom dancing derived from the traditional Standard dances (e.g., Waltz, Fox Trot, Tango), in which the partners are free to release each other from the closed embrace and dance without any physical contact, thus permitting improvisation and individual expression.

FOX TROT FRIDAYS

*Do you think you could possibly behave
a little less like yourself?*

ALL SOULS'

Starting up behind them,
all the voices of those they had named:
mink, gander, and marmoset,
crow and cockatiel.
Even the duck-billed platypus,
of late so quiet in its bed,
sent out a feeble cry signifying
grief and confusion, et cetera.

Of course the world had changed
for good. As it would from now on
every day, with every twitch and blink.
Now that change was de rigueur,
man would discover desire, then yearn
for what he would learn to call
distraction. This was the true loss.
And yet in that first

unchanging instant,
the two souls
standing outside the gates
(no more than a break in the hedge;
how had they missed it?) were not
thinking. Already the din was fading.
Before them, a silence
larger than all their ignorance

yawned, and this they walked into
until it was all they knew. In time
they hunkered down to business,
filling the world with sighs—
these anonymous, pompous creatures,
heads tilted as if straining
to make out the words to a song
played long ago, in a foreign land.

"I HAVE BEEN A STRANGER IN A STRANGE LAND"

Life's spell is so exquisite, everything
conspires to break it.
          —EMILY DICKINSON

It wasn't bliss. What was bliss
but the ordinary life? She'd spend hours
in patter, moving through whole days
touching, sniffing, tasting . . . exquisite
housekeeping in a charmed world.
And yet there was always

more of the same, all that happiness,
the aimless Being There.
So she wandered for a while, bush to arbor,
lingered to look through a pond's restive mirror.
He was off cataloging the universe, probably,
pretending he could organize
what was clearly someone else's chaos.

That's when she found the tree,
the dark, crabbed branches
bearing up such speechless bounty,
she knew without being told
this was forbidden. It wasn't
a question of ownership—
who could lay claim to
such maddening perfection?

And there was no voice in her head,
no whispered intelligence lurking
in the leaves—just an ache that grew
until she knew she'd already lost everything
except desire, the red heft of it
warming her outstretched palm.

FOX TROT FRIDAYS

Thank the stars there's a day
each week to tuck in

the grief, lift your pearls, and
stride brush stride

quick-quick with a
heel-ball-toe. Smooth

as Nat King Cole's
slow satin smile,

easy as taking
one day at a time:

one man and
one woman,

rib to rib,
with no heartbreak in sight—

just the sweep of Paradise
and the space of a song

to count all the wonders in it.

TA TA CHA CHA

One, two—no, five doves
scatter before a wingtip's
distracted tread.
Lost, lost, they coo, and
they're probably right:
It's Venice, I'm American,
besandaled and backpacked,
sunk in a bowl of sky

trimmed with marbled statuary
(slate, snow, ash)—
a dazed array, dipped
in the moon's cold palette.

Who, you? No. But here,
lost from a wing, drifts
one pale, italicized
answer. I pick it up
as the bold shoe
continues conversation
(*one two*) with its mate,
and the nearest scavenger
skips three times
to the side, bobs to pluck
his crackerjack prize, a child's
dropped gelato cone.

Tip, tap: early warning code
for afternoon rain. Gray
vagabond, buffoon messenger
for grounded lovers—where to?
Teach me this dance
you make, snatching a sweet
from the path of a man
who, because he knows
where he's headed, walks
without seeing, face hidden
by a dirty wingspan
of the daily news.

QUICK

Look, a baby one! Wink of fuzz
in the headlights, and gray at that.

Now he peers from the culvert,
all bobble and twitch, vacant eyes:

he's been through this bait and switch
all night. *Where's mother?*

On the hill, there—crested
in moonshine the fabled silhouette,

sleek curve plumpening into a tail
waving its flamboyant

afterthought, she disappears:
red swish

or gray, too quick to tell.
O to be gone

like that, no grief nor thought
of love—pure purpose

poured into flight.

BROWN

Why you look good in every color!
the dress lady gurgled, just before
I stepped onto the parquet
for a waltz. I demurred;
we were in a country club,
after all, and she—fresh
from Fort Lauderdale (do people
actually live there?) with five
duffel bags' worth of ball gowns,
enough tulle and fringe and pearls
to float a small cotillion—
was only trying to earn a living.
For once I was not the only
black person in the room
(two others, both male).
I thought of Sambo; I thought

a few other things, too,
unmentionable here. Don't
get me wrong: I've always loved
my skin, the way it glows against
citron and fuchsia, the difficult hues,
but the difference I cause
whenever I walk into a polite space
is why I prefer grand entrances—
especially with a Waltz,
that European constipated
swoon.

The dress in question was red.

FOX

She knew what
she was and so
was capable
of anything
anyone
could imagine.
She loved what
she was, there
for the taking,
imagine.

She imagined
nothing.
She loved
nothing more
than what she had,
which was enough
for her,
which was more
than any man
could handle.

HEART TO HEART

It's neither red
nor sweet.
It doesn't melt
or turn over,
break or harden,
so it can't feel
pain,
yearning,
regret.

It doesn't have
a tip to spin on,
it isn't even
shapely—
just a thick clutch
of muscle,
lopsided,
mute. Still,
I feel it inside
its cage sounding
a dull tattoo:
I want, I want—

but I can't open it:
there's no key.
I can't wear it
on my sleeve,
or tell you from
the bottom of it
how I feel. Here,
it's all yours, now—
but you'll have
to take me,
too.

COZY APOLOGÍA
—for Fred

I could pick anything and think of you—
This lamp, the wind-still rain, the glossy blue
My pen exudes, drying matte, upon the page.
I could choose any hero, any cause or age
And, sure as shooting arrows to the heart,
Astride a dappled mare, legs braced as far apart
As standing in silver stirrups will allow—
There you'll be, with furrowed brow
And chain mail glinting, to set me free:
One eye smiling, the other firm upon the enemy.

This post-post-modern age is all business: compact disks
And faxes, a do-it-now-and-take-no-risks
Event. Today a hurricane is nudging up the coast,
Oddly male: Big Bad Floyd, who brings a host
Of daydreams: awkward reminiscences
Of teenage crushes on worthless boys
Whose only talent was to kiss you senseless.
They all had sissy names—Marcel, Percy, Dewey;
Were thin as licorice and as chewy,
Sweet with a dark and hollow center. Floyd's

Cussing up a storm. You're bunkered in your
Aerie, I'm perched in mine
(Twin desks, computers, hardwood floors):
We're content, but fall short of the Divine.
Still, it's embarrassing, this happiness—
Who's satisfied simply with what's good for us,
When has the ordinary ever been news?
And yet, because nothing else will do
To keep me from melancholy (call it blues),
I fill this stolen time with you.

SOPRANO

When you hit
the center

of a note, spin
through and off

the bell lip
into heaven,

the soul dies
for an instant—

but you don't need
its thin

resistance
nor the room

(piano shawl,
mirror, hyacinth)

dissolving
as one note

pours into
the next, pebbles

clean as moonspill
seeding a path . . .

and which is it,
body or mind,

which rises, which
gives up at last

and goes home?

TWO FOR THE MONTROSE DRIVE-IN

TUPPERWARE

Three days before it was pick-up-and-scrub,
the tops of doorjambs wiped clean
for white gloves come to test disarray.

Dad packed up us kids and fled
the cheddar cubes, plastic forks suspended
in Jell-O—*that* was judgment, ambrosia and trident—

oh, but it was delicious
at the Drive-In, sliding in pajamas down
into the pit, waking

just in time to see
great Pharaoh drowned
and Charlton Heston rosy

in his holy rags . . . now, that
was a good story, that
kept us awake

until the end credits, the moon
huge as it wandered down
the black gullet of avenue,

bright eye swallowing
the windshield. . . . We made it
home to the ruins

of the feast: crustless sandwiches
smelling faintly of ocean, platoons
of celery, mints and dip (they always

finished the cake), a soggy lemon
crescent lolling in the red bottom
of the drained punch bowl,

and the house a mess. We ate like kings for days.

CHARLTON HESTON'S HOLY RAGS

Our lucky man puts in his first appearance.
We cheer, ski the front seat vinyl
into the plushy pit beneath the dash.

Just as sure as we're missing the chalky mints
discretely placed between the moistened lips
of the Reverend Sisters of the Eastern Star,

he'll save us from plopping frogs or locusts,

clouds of hissing *told-you-sos*
invading bed or pajama cuff.

This time around, though, he's neither
good nor wise: He tromps palatial corridors,
a smooth-cheeked boy in Roman bronze,

all greed and good looks.
No green smoke wriggling over a host of snakes
ready to be turned into walking sticks;

instead, he lifts his hand and an urn,
kicked, stutters across the tiles:
The car speaker crackles scorn.

What brand of righteousness is this? Squeamish,
we stuff our mouths with more buttered corn
and count the things gone wrong—

there's a sister rotting away in a cave,
too many sweaty people being whipped,
that skinny stranger's burning gaze . . .

and then, just when we begin to doubt him,
we watch as doubt struggles up to crouch
inside his own baby blues. Oh,

now he rises to his chiseled best,
takes redemption's arrow
deep into his manly chest

as rain comes down in torrents,
lightning timed to tell each flash of news
(the rock rolled back, the lepers' new-washed skin),

and through it all—the tears, the flood,
Thy Kingdom Come in gold
and cobalt streaks—he stands aglow

with Blessedness, with . . . could it be
remorse? Whatever for?—and in
an instant, he suddenly

grows old.

MEDITATION AT FIFTY YARDS, MOVING TARGET

Safety First.

Never point your weapon, keep your finger
off the trigger. Assume a loaded barrel,
even when it isn't, especially when you *know* it isn't.
Glocks are lightweight but sensitive;
the Keltec has a long pull and a kick.
Rifles have penetrating power, viz.:
if the projectile doesn't lodge in its mark,
it will travel some distance
until it finds shelter; it will certainly
pierce your ordinary drywall partition.
You could wound the burglar and kill your child
sleeping in the next room, all with one shot.

Open Air.

Fear, of course. Then the sudden
pleasure of heft—as if the hand
had always yearned for this solemn
fit, this *gravitas*, and now had found
its true repose.

Don't pull the trigger, squeeze it—
squeeze between heartbeats.
Look down the sights. Don't
hold your breath. Don't hold
anything, just stop breathing.
Level the scene with your eyes. Listen.
Soft, now: squeeze.

Gender Politics.

Guys like noise: rapid fire,
thunk-and-slide of a blunt-nose silver Mossberg
or double-handed Colts, slugging it out from the hips.
Rambo or cowboy, they'll whoop it up.

Women are fewer, more elegant.
They prefer precision:
tin cans swing-dancing in the trees,
the paper bull's-eye's tidy rupture at fifty yards.

> (Question: If you were being pursued,
>   how would you prefer to go down—
>   ripped through a blanket of fire
>   or plucked by one incandescent
> fingertip?)

The Bullet.

dark dark no wind no heaven
i am not anything not borne on air i bear
myself i can slice the air no wind
can hold me let me let me

go i can see yes
o aperture o light let me off
go off straight is my verb straight
my glory road yes now i can feel
it the light i am flame velocity o
beautiful body i am coming i am yours
before you know it
i am home

AMERICAN SMOOTH

We were dancing—it must have
been a foxtrot or a waltz,
something romantic but
requiring restraint,
rise and fall, precise
execution as we moved
into the next song without
stopping, two chests heaving
above a seven-league
stride—such perfect agony
one learns to smile through,
ecstatic mimicry
being the *sine qua non*
of American Smooth.
And because I was distracted
by the effort of
keeping my frame
(the leftward lean, head turned
just enough to gaze out
past your ear and always
smiling, smiling),
I didn't notice
how still you'd become until
we had done it
(for two measures?
four?)—achieved flight,

that swift and serene
magnificence,
before the earth
remembered who we were
and brought us down.

NOT WELCOME HERE

*You may find nobility in the savage, Commander,
but he is only interested in killing you.*

THE CASTLE WALK

(*New York City, 1915. James Reese Europe, bandleader.*)

You can't accuse this group
of havin' too much mustard—
they're gloved and buttoned

tighter than Buddy's snare drum.
But they're paying, so
we pay 'em back—pour on

the violins, insinuate
a little cello,
lay some grizzly piano

under that sweet jelly roll.
Our boys got a snap and buzz
no one dancing

in this gauze and tinsel
showroom knows how
to hear: The couples stroll

past, counting to themselves
as they orbit, chins poked out
as if expecting a kiss or

in need of a shave; we pitch
and surge through each ragtime
and I swear, it's both

luck and hardship,
the way the music
slips as it burns.

These white folks stalk
through privilege
just like they dance:

one-two, stop, pose,
over and over.
We ain't nobody

special, but at least we know it:
Across the black Atlantic,
they're trampling up the map

into a crazy quilt of rage
and honor; here,
the biggest news going

would be Irene and Vernon
teaching the Castle Walk.
(Trot on, Irene! Vernon, fake that

juke joint slide.) So boys,
lay down tracks, the old world's
torched; we'll ride this train as far

as it's going. Let's kick it:
Time for the Innovation Tango!
Buddy, set 'em marching;

and you, Mr. Cricket Smith—mortify 'em
with your cornet's
molten silver moan!

THE PASSAGE
(*Corporal Orval E. Peyton, 372nd Infantry, 93rd Division, A.E.F.*)

Saturday, March 30, 1917

                                    Got up
this morning at 2:45, breakfast at 3:30,
a beautiful sky, warm, and the moon bright.
I slept in my clothes, overcoat and socks.

I was restless last night, listening to the others
moving about.

Now, all the boys seem cheerful.
This will be a day never to be forgotten.
After breakfast—beef stew and coffee—
Charlie and I cleaned up the rest of the mail.

~

It is now 4:30 in the afternoon.
The whistle has blown for us
and everybody ordered down off deck.

I am not worried; I am anxious to go.

This morning we left camp at 7 and marched
silently along the town's perimeter to port.
No cheering nor tears shed, no one
to see us off, to kiss and cry over.
F company was leading. I looked back at
several hundred men
marching toward they knew not what.
When we passed through the lower end of the city
a few colored people
stood along the street, watching.
One lady raised her apron to wipe away a tear.

I turned my head to see how the fellow next to me,
Corporal Crawford from Massachusetts,
was taking it. Our eyes met and we both smiled.
Not that we thought it was funny, but—
we were soldiers.
There were more things in this world
than a woman's tears.

~

March 31

>Easter Sunday.
I was up to services held by a chaplain
but am not feeling well enough to get something to eat.
All the boys are gathered around the hatch
singing "My Little Girl." Talked to a sailor
who's been across twice; he says this ship
has had four battles with subs, each time
beating them off.

This boat is named *The Susquehanna*—
German built, interned before
the U.S. declared war. Her old name was *The Rhine*.
The other ship that left Newport News with us
was known as *Prinz Friedrich*.

We pulled out last night at 5
and I soon went to bed, so tired
I nearly suffocated, for I had left off my fan.
(We sleep in bunks three high and two
side by side with no ventilation
in quarters situated near the steam room.
The stair straight down. Everything in steel.)

April 1 (All Fools' Day)

>Nothing but water.
Just back from breakfast, home-style:
sausage, potatoes and gravy, oatmeal, coffee, bread
and an apple. The food seems better here than
in camp. Our boys do not complain much.

The sailors say we are the jolliest bunch of fellows
they have ever taken across. This boat's been over
twice before and according to them
this trip is the charm—either
the ship will be sunk or it will be good for the war.

I guess we are bound to have trouble, for it is said
the submarines are busy in this kind of weather.

Last night I could not eat all my supper, so went on deck.
No moon out but the sky full of stars,
and I remember thinking
The future will always be with me.
About 7 o'clock I saw a few lights some distance ahead
a little to the left. The boat made toward them;
as we drew nearer I recognized a red beacon.
Our gunners got busy and trained the sights.
We passed within 500 yards.
The stern was all lit. Someone said
it was a hospital ship.

     ᔋ

April 2, Tuesday

               Good breakfast—
bacon, eggs, grits, and of course coffee.
We ran into ships ahead about an hour ago.
I can see four, probably the rest of the fleet.

Most of the boys are on deck. A few are down here
playing blackjack and poker, and the band's playing, too.
I've been on deck all morning, up on a beam
trying to read the semaphore.

5:30 p.m. Just had supper. We ate with F Company
tonight: potatoes, corned beef, apple butter and coffee.
We've overtaken the other ships; I can see four more
to our ports. I got wet on deck about an hour ago.

I can hear the waves splashing! I think
I'll go up and smoke before it gets dark.

     ᔋ

April 3, Wednesday

Just came down
off deck; the sea is high and waves all over.
I put on my raincoat to get in them—great sport!
There were six ships to our ports and a battleship starboard.

4 p.m. The storm is rocking us so,
no one can stay on deck without getting soaked.
I have been in my bunk all afternoon.

Quite a few of the boys are sick by now.
I feel a trifle dizzy;
there's something wrong with the ship,
I don't know what it is, but they called for
all the pipe fitters they could find.
Some of the boys have put on life preservers
but most don't seem to be afraid and are as jolly
as if they were on shore. Some say
they don't think we'll make it.
We are some kind of circus down here.

    ~

7 p.m.: our ship gets a wireless every evening
telling us the war news. Ever since supper
there has been a bunch on deck laughing,
singing, and dancing. A large wave swept
over the planks and drenched us all but
the stronger the sea, the more noise we made.
At last, just as Pickney had finished
a mock speech with "I thank you, ladies and gentlemen,"
a larger wave poured a foot of water on deck.

The sailors had crowded around us; they say
pity the Germans when a bunch like us hit them.

    ~

April 4, Thursday

> Fifth day out.
I'm feeling all right—that is,
I don't feel like I did when I was on land,
but I am not sick. Last night I couldn't go to sleep
for a long while in that hot hole.
About 4 a.m., I put on my slippers
and went up for a breath of air.
The storm had passed and stars were shining,
half a dozen sailors busy with ropes.
One of the guards instructed me to close
my slicker, for my white underclothes were glowing.

Everybody this morning was in good spirits
and the deck was crowded with our boys.
Calm sea, a fair breeze blowing.
At ten o'clock we had "Abandon Ship" drill:
we were ordered below to our bunks
to put on life preservers, then
a whistle blew, some petty officers yelled
"all hands abandon ship," and we went
quickly to our places on the raft.
There are twenty-five of us in a boat.
My boat's number one.

᠊ᡒ

When I think that I am a thousand miles
from land, in the middle of the Ocean,
I am not a bit impressed as I imagined I would be.
Things have certainly changed. A year ago
I was sitting in school, studying.
I had never been out of the state of Ohio
and never gone from home for more than
two weeks at a time. Now I'm away
eight months—four in the Deep South,
four in Virginia and now
on the High Seas.
I wonder where I'll be this time next year.

April 5, Friday

             Last night after dinner
I started reading a book borrowed from Crawford
titled *Life of the Immortal.* Stopped
long enough for supper, and finished it
about an hour ago. Then with Shelton,
Davis, and Crawford, talked about literature.
I didn't get to bed before 10 o'clock
and did not feel like getting up this morning.

It is very hard to obtain soap on board
that will lather in salt water.
I can't get my hands clean without soap; but
one of the sailors gave me a piece
that's pretty good. So far I have managed
to stay fresh but some of the dudes don't care
and their hands are awful looking.
I haven't shaved since I've been
on board; I won't shave
until land is in sight.

April 6, Saturday

             Wrestling match
with Casey; I was wet with sweat when we stopped
and went on deck to cool off.
We're served just two meals a day now, 9 and 3 o'clock.
Rich Tuggle and others bought a lot of cakes and candy
from the canteen, so I was too full to eat supper.

This morning in the mess line
Rick spotted some kind of large fish near our boat.
All I saw was its tail, but it shot up water
like I've seen in pictures in school.

A whale, I thought, *maybe it's a whale!*
But it went under without a noise.

～

April 7, Sunday

We had a death
on board last night, a cook by the name of Bibbie.
Chaplain Nelson held the service
on the other end of the boat.
Mess call sounded before he had finished.
(Pork, potatoes, corn and coffee.)

This is an ideal Sunday afternoon;
I wonder what we would be doing back home
if I was there. Now I will read awhile
and then lie down. I am tired of the voyage.
I suppose there are lonesome days before me,
but no more so than those that have already passed.
I can make myself contented.
We are having very good weather.

It must have been a whale!

NOBLE SISSLE'S HORN

(Northern France / Spartansburg, South Carolina. The 369th.)

A cornet's soul is in its bell—
trap that liquid gasp
and you're cooking.

> *(Take your hat off, boy.*
> *Not quick enough.*
> *Pick it up! Too slow.)*

A horn needs to choke on
what feeds it, it has to want
the air to sing out.

Nigger, where you been raised?
This is a respectable establishment.

The difference between a moan and a hallelujah
ain't much of a slide.
I don't know how I knew this,
growing up deep in the church
deep in Indianapolis—

> *Bent over like a mule*
> *from one bitty kick—why,*
> *you need strengthening.*

but right now, standing here itching
up under all this wool, I figure:

> *What you staring at?*
> *You got something to say?*

When you've got whole nations lining up
just to mow each other down—hell,
a man can hoot just as well as holler.

ALFONZO PREPARES TO GO OVER THE TOP
(*Belleau Wood, 1917*)

"A soldier waits until he's called—then
moves ass and balls up, over,
tearing twigs and crushed faces,
swinging his bayonet like a pitchfork
and thinking *anything's better*
than a trench, ratshit
and the tender hairs of chickweed.
A soldier is smoke
waiting for wind; he's a long corridor
clanging to the back of a house
where a child sings
in its ruined nursery . . .

and Beauty is the

gleam of my eye on this gunstock and my spit
drying on the blade of this knife
before it warms itself in the gut of a Kraut.
Mother, forgive me. Hear the leaves? I am
already memory."

LA CHAPELLE. 92ND DIVISION. TED.

(*September, 1918*)

This lonely beautiful word
                              means church
and it is quiet here; the stone
walls curve
                    like slow water.
When we arrived the people were already gone,
green shutters latched and stoops swept clean.
A cow lowed through the village,
pushing into our gloves her huge
sodden jaw.

It's Sunday and I'm standing
on the bitter ridge of France, overlooking the war.
La Guerre is asleep. This morning early
on patrol we slipped down through
the mist and scent of burning woodchips
(somewhere someone was warm)
                              into Moyenmoutier,
cloister of flushed brick and a little river
braiding its dark hair.

Back home in Louisiana the earth is red,
but it suckles you until you can sing
yourself grown.
                    Here, even the wind has edges.
Drizzle splintered around us; we stood
on the arched bridge and thought
for a moment of the dead we had left
behind in the valley, in the terrible noise.

But I'm not sad—on the way back
through the twigs I glimpsed
in a broken windowbox by the roadside
mums:
stunned lavenders and pinks
dusted with soot.
                        I am a little like them,
heavy-headed,
rough curls open to the rain.

VARIATION ON RECLAMATION

(*Aix-les-Bains, 1918. Teddy.*)

Coming To.

      Music across the lake? Impossible . . .
      it had to be coming from behind him,
      doughboys in the square, catching some rays,

      Calvin's piccolo tickling the air.
      He'd let it ride, just a little while . . .

2nd Waking.

      Every morning tap-step, tap-step
      from cot to veranda, then lean

      against the doorframe, head back
      to feel the dew. *All right: Ready?*

      Elbow cocked (*yes*) to push
      the forearm through the sleeve

      (*check*), jacket hunched up and
      over (*hoopla!*)—to do at least

      this much!—brought tears. *Good work,*
      they'd say; *why don't you rest a bit?*

For the walk back, they mean.
The sun on his cheek, a gentle burn.

Setback. Bedrest.

How could he recover without a song?
His whistle tuckered, voice cracked
into a thousand rasps and throttles.

No tin cup, but here's a hook to keep him
in line—silver curve too ornery

to strum or take bets with,
lift a caramel chin for a kiss . . .

Dismissal.

He'd been to the mountain
and found it green and trembling

with its fallen. He'd called out
so many times to those lost last breaths

it was like listening to his own heart
—flutter, stop, kick, canter—

all in a day's climb. The stick
wasn't there for decoration:

he'd own it, old man tottering
out of hellfire, a medal bumping

his chest (*step, tap*), at his back
an impertinent nation

popping gum as they jeered: *Boy,*
we told you to watch your step.

THE RETURN OF LIEUTENANT JAMES REESE EUROPE

(*Victory Parade, New York City, February 1919*)

We trained in the streets: the streets where we came from.
We drilled with sticks, boys darting between bushes, shouting—
that's all you thought we were good for. We trained anyway.
In camp we had no plates or forks. First to sail, first to join the French,
first to see combat with the shortest training time.

My, the sun is looking fine today.

We toured devastation, American good will
in a forty-four piece band. Dignitaries smiled; the wounded
settled back to dream. That old woman in St. Nazaire
who tucked up her skirts so she could "walk the dog."
German prisoners tapping their feet as we went by.

Miss Flatiron with your tall cool self: How do.

You didn't want us when we left but we went.
You didn't want us coming back but here we are,
stepping right up white-faced Fifth Avenue in a phalanx
(*no prancing, no showing of teeth, no swank*)
past the Library lions, eyes forward, tin hats aligned—

a massive, upheld human shield.

No jazz for you: We'll play a brisk French march
and show our ribbons, flash our *Croix de Guerre*
(yes, we learned French, too) all the way
until we reach 110th Street and yes! take our turn
onto Lenox Avenue and all those brown faces and then—

Baby, Here Comes Your Daddy Now!

RIPONT

The men helped clear the enemy out of Bussy Farm,
advanced toward Ripont, and were in the fighting at Sechault;
then they were pulled back to Bussy Farm. In these actions
they captured sixty of the enemy, and equipment including
several artillery and antitank weapons.

Early fall in the fields a slow day's drive south
of Paris French birds singing frenchly enough
though we didn't know their names in any language—
not even the German of my husband
reared in a village like the one we were passing
in our rusty orange BMW   baby daughter
crowing from the backseat her plastic shell
strapped over the cracked upholstery

We were *en route* to the battlefields of the 369th
the Great War's Negro Soldiers
who it was said fought like tigers
joking as the shells fell around them
so that the French told the Americans
Send us more like these and they did and so
the Harlem Hellfighters earned their stripes
in the War To End All Wars

We followed cow paths bisected pastures
barreled down stretches of gravel arrow straight
until the inevitable curve signaling each hamlet
noonday silence dreary stone barns and a few
crooked houses cobblestones boiling up
under our wheels the air thick with flies
the sky streaked cream stirred in a cup

The maps we'd bought in Montparnasse were exquisite
Each dry creek bed and fallow square
each warped stile or cracked fountain appeared
at the appointed millimeter under my index finger
This afternoon the battlefield at Ripont
one more name in a string of villages
destroyed during the course of their own salvation

We were thrilled when the copse of oaks
appeared on the left just as the five dots printed
in the crease of the Michelin had predicted
we counted the real trees to see if there were five
of them too but there were seven   Down an embankment

then to the blue squiggle denoting a stream
our daughter gurgling her pleasure as I reached back
to feed her another spoonful of Gerber's spinach
cold from the jar   A sharp right
onto the map's dotted line   Two tire tracks
leading into deeper foliage path blotted by vines
the sun a cottony blur too far off to help us
through locked branches a sudden rectangle yellow and black
ACHTUNG – MINEN   watch out for mines

This was the village before that September
decades ago before victory ploughed through
leaving her precocious seeds   Past
the brambles the broken staves of barbed wire
we could see a frayed doorway a keystone
frame of a house gone a-kilter
like a child's smudged crayon drawing

A branch slapped the windshield I shrieked
rolled up the windows as if tragedy were
contagious as if our daughter could detonate
the mines by tossing her rattle into the briars
We were in deep no way out except by
shifting in reverse so we drove on till at last
there came a clearing a crabgrass mound
choked under a layer of gleaming automobiles

Nothing to do but park so we pulled behind
a Peugeot got out and followed the road
on foot turning a bend onto a smattering
of people decked out in their somber best
some older ladies with corsages some with veils
a lean man with the hat and mustache of a mayor
was giving a speech   We made out

the year of the battle the name of the town
a bugle sounded as two old soldiers laid down a wreath
and only then did we notice the memorial stone
with the date   today's   and the names of the fallen
both the French and the Negro

Everyone smiled at us sadly they thought
we were descendants too
What else could we do we smiled back
we let them believe we drove with the crowd
single file through the woods to the river
where we turned left they turned right
some of them waving
our daughter waving back
We kept on until twilight stopped us
found an inn in a town not starred on our map
where I sat in a room at a small wooden table
by the side of our bed and wrote nothing
for thirteen years not a word in my notebook
until today

for Aviva, leaving home

TWELVE CHAIRS

My logic was not in error, but I was.

FIRST JUROR

Proof casts a shadow;
doubt is to walk
onto a field
at high noon
one tendril
held to
the
wind.

SECOND JUROR

A stone to throw

A curse to hurl

A silence to break

A page to write

A day to live

A blank

To fill

THIRD JUROR

between the lip
and the kiss
between the hand
and the fist
between rumor
and prayer
between dungeon
and tower
between fear
and liberty
always
between

FOURTH JUROR

Cancel the afternoon
evenings mornings all
the days to come
until the fires
fall to ash
the fog clears
and we can see
where we
really
stand.

FIFTH JUROR

How long will
this take?
I am not my
brother,
thank you;
my hands are
full already
taking care
of
myself.

SIXTH JUROR

I'm not anyone more
than anyone else.
I did my job, then
looked into
their eyes.
What had I
become?

SEVENTH JUROR

In the mind of the crow
burns a golden cry   In
the heart of the mole
an endless sky   In
the eye of the trout
shines a galaxy
And I who see this
tell no one
I who am
a corridor
longing
to be
field

EIGHTH JUROR

Look around:
magic everywhere.
Behind you,
tears and shadow.
Ahead the path
clean flame.
Look up, the air
is singing:
Underfoot
your shadow
waits.

NINTH JUROR

Not the eyes—never
look into the eyes.
The soul either
strikes out
or
trembles
beneath
the blow.

TENTH JUROR

Tragedy
involves
one.
History
involves many
toppling
one
after
another.

ELEVENTH JUROR

You can't mop the floor
before the milk's
been spilled;
you can't run off
if your shadow
is pinned
to
the wall.

TWELFTH JUROR

why is the rose
how is the sun
where is first
when is last
who will
love us
what
will
save
us

THE ALTERNATE

—And who are you?
—*Nobody.*
—What do you do?
—*I am alive.*
—But who'll vouch
for you?
—*Listen closely,*
you'll hear
the
wind.

BLUES IN HALF-TONES, 3/4 TIME

[Our] heart was forged out of barbarism and violence. We learned to control it, but it is still a part of us. To pretend it does not exist is to create an opportunity for it to escape.

CHOCOLATE

Velvet fruit, exquisite square
I hold up to sniff
between finger and thumb—

how you numb me
with your rich attentions!
If I don't eat you quickly,

you'll melt in my palm.
Pleasure seeker, if I let you
you'd liquefy everywhere.

Knotted smoke, dark punch
of earth and night and leaf,
for a taste of you

any woman would gladly
crumble to ruin.
Enough chatter: I am ready

to fall in love!

BOLERO

Not the ratcheting crescendo of Ravel's bright winds
but an older,
crueler

passion: a woman with hips who knows when to move them,
who holds nothing back
but the hurt

she takes with her as she dips, grinds, then rises sweetly into
his arms again.
Not

delicate. Not tame. Bessie Smith in a dream of younger,
(*Can't you see?*)
slimmer

days. Restrained in the way a debutante is not, the way a bride
pretends she
understands.

How everything hurts! Each upsurge onto a throbbing toe,
the prolonged descent
to earth,

to him (*what love & heartache done to me*), her body ferocious,
a grim ululation
of flesh—

she adores him. And he savors that adoration, this man in love
                                                with looking.
She feels his look,
his sigh

and she moves, moves with him to the music in the space
                                                allotted them,
spot lit across
the hardwood floor.

HATTIE MCDANIEL ARRIVES AT
   THE COCONUT GROVE

late, in aqua and ermine, gardenias
scaling her left sleeve in a spasm of scent,
her gloves white, her smile chastened, purse giddy
with stars and rhinestones clipped to her brilliantined hair,
on her free arm that fine Negro,
Mr. Wonderful Smith.

It's the day that isn't, February 29th,
at the end of the shortest month of the year—

and the shittiest, too, everywhere
except Hollywood, California,
where the maid can wear mink and still be a maid,
bobbing her bandaged head and cursing
the white folks under her breath as she smiles
and shoos their silly daughters
in from the night dew . . . what can she be
thinking of, striding into the ballroom
where no black face has ever showed itself
except above a serving tray?

Hi-Hat Hattie, Mama Mac, Her Haughtiness,
the "little lady" from *Showboat* whose name
Bing forgot, Beulah & Bertha & Malena
& Carrie & Violet & Cynthia & Fidelia,
one half of the Dark Barrymores—
dear Mammy we can't help but hug you crawl into
your generous lap tease you
with arch innuendo so we can feel that
much more wicked and youthful
and sleek but oh what

we forgot: the four husbands, the phantom
pregnancy, your famous parties, your celebrated
ice box cake. Your giggle above the red petticoat's rustle,
black girl and white girl walking hand in hand
down the railroad tracks
in Kansas City, six years old.
The man who advised you, now
that you were famous, to "begin eliminating"
your more "common" acquaintances
and your reply (catching him square
in the eye): "That's a good idea.
I'll start right now by eliminating you."

Is she or isn't she? Three million dishes,
a truckload of aprons and headrags later, and here
you are: poised, between husbands
and factions, no corset wide enough
to hold you in, your huge face a dark moon split

by that spontaneous smile—your trademark,
your curse. No matter, Hattie: It's a long, beautiful walk
into that flower-smothered standing ovation,
so go on
and make them wait.

SAMBA SUMMER

Fort Valley, Georgia, 1966

Broke-leg cakewalk of the drunken uncles
entertaining the ladies at the family picnic:
one arm akimbo in a humpback strut,
the other stretched high in witness—*yes, Lord, yes!*—
palm outspread against a late summer sky.

> *That skirt's too yellow*
> *and far too tight*
> *for any Christian child.*
> *I'd walk a mile*
> *if the gal was right*
> *but those hips could kill a fellow!*

One straight leg, too, that the crooked one dragged
through a grassy rut edging the petunias.
The women rolled their eyes, clucked
the children away from the charred hibachi,
and set out the coconut cream pies.

> *You may as well*
> *go on and shoot me,*
> *tie my heart in a knot.*
> *Wait: judging from*
> *this limp here,*
> *my leg's already shot!*

High-butt shenanigans! Uncles did it best,
pot-gutted, hitching their trousers up—
a holy grunting executed to the bleat and hiss

of Mitzi's seafoam green transistor,
comic signature of the tribe:

> *We're only joking: we know*
> *we're just the world's*
> *custodians, full-time lovers*
> *on half pay. C'mon, girl,*
> *let's dance—before this song is over,*
> *show me what I've been working for.*

BLUES IN HALF-TONES, 3/4 TIME

From nothing comes nothing,
don't you know that by now?
Not a thing for you, sweet thing,
not a wing nor a prayer,
though you got half
by birthright,
itching under the skin.

(There's a typo somewhere.)
Buck 'n' wing,
common prayer—
which way do you run?
The oaken bucket's
all busted
and the water's all gone.

I'm not for sale because I'm free.
(So they say. They say
the play's the thing, too,
but we *know* that don't play.)
Everyone's a ticket
or a stub, so it might as well
cost you, my dear.

But are you sure you lost it?
Did you check the back seat?

What a bitch. Gee, that sucks.
Well, you know what they say.
What's gone's gone.
No use crying.
(There's a moral *some*where.)

DESCRIBE YOURSELF IN THREE WORDS OR LESS

I'm not the kind of person who praises
openly, or for profit; I'm not the kind
who will steal a scene unless
I've designed it. I'm not a kind at all,
in fact: I'm itchy and pug-willed,
gnarled and wrong-headed,
never amorous but possessing
a wild, thatched soul.

Each night I set my boats to sea
and leave them to their bawdy business.
Whether they drift off
maddened, moon-rinsed,
or dock in the morning
scuffed and chastened—
is simply how it is, and I gather them in.

You are mine, I say to the twice-dunked cruller
before I eat it. Then I sing
to the bright-beaked bird outside,
then to the manicured spider
between window and screen;
then I will stop, and forget the singing.
(See? I have already forgotten you.)

THE SEVEN VEILS OF SALOMÉ

Salomé Awaits Her Entrance.

> I was standing in the doorway
> when he reproached her.
> Not with words, but a simple
> absence of attention: She was smiling,
> holding out a slip of meat, skewered fruit—
> some delicacy he'd surely never seen
> in all his dust-blown, flea-plagued
> wanderings—and he stared at it
> for the longest while,
> as if the offer came from it and not
> those tapered fingers, my mother's
> famous smile. He said nothing,
> merely turned away his large
> and beautifully arrogant head.

Herodias, in the Doorway.

> More than anything I ache to see her
> so girlish. She steps languidly
> into their midst as if onto a pooled expanse
> of grass . . . or as if she were herself
> the meadow, unruffled green
> ringed with lilies
> instead of these red-rimmed eyes,
> this wasteland soaked in smoke and pleasure.
> Ignorant, she moves as if inventing
> time—and the musicians scurry
> to deliver a carpet of flutes
> under her flawless heel.

Herod, Watching.

> I should have avoided this, loving her mother
> as I do, to the length and breadth of my kingdom,
> even to the chilly depths of history's wrath.
> But it was my birthday; I was bent upon

happiness and love, I loved
Herodias, my Herodias!—who sends
her honeyed daughter into the feast.
The first veil fell, and all
my celebrated years
dissolved in bitter rapture. O Herodias!
You have outdone us all.

The Fool, at Herod's Feet.

Just a girl, slim-hipped, two knots
for breasts, sheathed potential
caught before the inevitable
over-bloom and rot (life's revenge
if death eludes us)—all
any of us men want, really.
Just a girl. Otherwise,
who can fathom it, how is it
to be fathomed? At his behest, her mother's?
It matters little—she was dispatched
into the circle of elders, and there
she rivets the world's desire.

Salomé, Dancing.

I have a head on my shoulders
but no one sees it; no one
reckons with a calculated wrist or pouting underlip.
I've navigated this court's attentions
and I will prove I can be crueler than government,
I will delegate what nature's given me
(this body, this anguish,
oiled curves and perfumed apertures),
I will dance until they've all lost their heads—
the nobles slobbering over their golden goblets,
the old king sweating on his throne,
my mother in the doorway, rigid with regret,
the jester who watches us all and laughs—

O Mother, what else is a girl to do?

FROM YOUR VALENTINE

(Valentinus, imprisoned.)

The days pass. Night floats,
continuous, a dark sheen in terror's
velvet grip. Is this what you
live in, dearest blind girl,
my jailor's daughter?
Like a shell whose portion of ocean
is constantly rocking,
keeping time, you carry
the cell of yourself
quietly. How else to locate
the anger in a tongue's *chk chk*,
the swift bite of his keys before
his hand slices the air? Outside

the city shouts, it growls and throbs.
You bring its hunger back
to whisper in my ear
and I write it down, ears burning—
all that pierced, burst, suppurating
anguish rendered into words,
hopeless scraps you slip
under your skirts, unabashed,
baring a thigh you cannot see.

Yet this sight does not stir me;
God's will is shameless. Only when
darkness swallows and you are all
around me and inside the dark—
O then I am most alive, spitted and turning,
and I dread . . . not pain,
snug in its own embrace, not
being without you, since I am
alone already—but the moment
before death, when pain and absence
blur, when I'll become
pure sensation.

I am calm when I can hear
your approach; I feel you
listening for me, my breathing
measured to your hurried step.
And when I speak, you lift
your entire body
into my voice, and I can look at you
all I want—I sin
over and over in gluttonous gazing,
your careful and thirsty face
a mirror
to my own. O my heart
is vigilant, hardened
to a single point it spins upon.
Martyrdom is easy:
I'll take the coward's path
and insist upon
my God, my righteous
love . . . until that love
snuffs out the man before you,
the one you see clearly,
who lives now
for the first time.

RHUMBA

yo vengo aquí	I come here
para cantar	to sing
la rumba	the rumba
de mi adoración	of my adoration

Wait.

                                            Here comes

At his touch

                                     the music:

(just under the tricep)

                          lean back, look at me—

lock your knees,

                              the straighter your legs

look, straight up

                the easier to fall,

into him, his hand stroking

                    to descend

your cheek. . . .

                          lightly.

Don't close your eyes.

                Don't bend your knees.

Let the body lift you

               Sigh upwards—trust me!

back on your feet.

                      Wait. Now

A touch again:

                      dip down

this time, twist

                but spread your arms;

in the knees,

                  give me some tone

but soft, follow (soft)

                    (more tone)

the reach, that last yearning

                  & connect. . . .

to his left wrist.

                Where's the audience?

Step forward.

                    Find them.

Rondé-hook-turn

                Let them see your face;

& reach again,

                now look for the stars,

reach, reach then

                    yes, keep

snap back—

                your elbow straight!

back to him,

                Here I am, &

always back to him. . . .

                here's your basic walk:

Ah, hips.

                  Enjoy it.

Quick-&-quick-

Hear the music? Enjoy it.

& slow . . .

Remember,

snake the right arm up,

after every turn

rock back &

find me &

dive, a swan,

shape,

head in the clouds

shoulders down——

then drop left,

keep going,

he'll catch you,

I've got you——

(good) to a right foot

quick quick now

slow:

relax.

Shape right,

Here comes the spiral;

kick back,

let me lead it.

yearn over him

C'mon, milk it, turn

to meet his thigh,

easy, easy . . .

ripple up his back.

don't settle.

Repeat on the left side.

Here's the check:

(Whew! That's over.)

beautiful line.

Rondé, pose:

Keep it tight, turn

quick-&-quick

(let me lead you)

knee up over &

——look at me,

lean, unwind & melt

                       find my eyes

toward him

                       so we can turn away

(straight legs) no—

                       in sync. & finally,

resist: *embrace:*

           my right your left
           my left your right
           your left his right
           your right his left

(don't cross your eyes)

                       look at me look deep

half spin to the right

                       forget the audience

stay on your toes now

                       lean into me,

define the length of him . . .

                       that's right . . .

the audience

                       forget them

the audience

                       your body

shuddering

                       all mine

into applause

                       now

THE SISTERS: SWANSONG.

We died one by one,
each plumper than the mirror
saw us. We exited obligingly,
rattling key chains and
cocktail jewelry, rehearsing
our ghostly encores.

Glad to be rid of pincurls
and prayers, bunions
burning between
ironed sheets—we sang
our laments, praised God
and went our way

quietly, were mourned
in satin and chrysanthemums,
whiskey and cake, old gossip
evaporating into cautionary tales.
Does it matter who went
first? Corinna or Fay,

heartache or coronary,
a reckless scalpel or
a careless life—whoever was left
kept count on the dwindling
rosary: Suzanna, Kit.
Mary. Violet. Pearl.

We all died of insignificance.

EVENING PRIMROSE

Proceed . . . carefully.

EVENING PRIMROSE

Poetically speaking, growing up is mediocrity.
—NED ROREM

Neither rosy nor prim,
not cousin to the cowslip
nor the extravagant fuchsia—
I doubt anyone has ever
picked one for show,
though the woods must be fringed
with their lemony effusions.

Sun blathers its baronial
endorsement, but they refuse
to join the ranks. Summer
brings them in armfuls,
yet, when the day is large,
you won't see them fluttering
the length of the road.

They'll wait until the world's
tucked in and the sky's
one ceaseless shimmer—then
lift their saturated eyelids
and blaze, blaze
all night long
for no one.

REVERIE IN OPEN AIR

I acknowledge my status as a stranger:
Inappropriate clothes, odd habits
Out of sync with wasp and wren.
I admit I don't know how
To sit still or move without purpose.
I prefer books to moonlight, statuary to trees.

But this lawn has been leveled for looking,
So I kick off my sandals and walk its cool green.
Who claims we're mere muscle and fluids?
My feet are the primitives here.
As for the rest—ah, the air now
Is a tonic of absence, bearing nothing
But news of a breeze.

SIC ITUR AD ASTRA

Thus is the way to the stars.
—VIRGIL

Bed, where are you flying to?
I went to sleep
nearly an hour ago,
and now I'm on a porch
open to the stars!

Close my eyes
and sink back to
day's tiny dismissals;
open wide and I'm
barefoot, nightshirt
fluttering white as a sail.

What will they say
when they find me
missing—just
the shape of my dreaming
creasing the sheets?
Come here, bed,

I need you! I don't know my way.
At least leave my pillow
behind to remind me
what affliction I've fled—
my poor, crushed pillow

with its garden of smells!

COUNT TO TEN AND WE'LL BE THERE

One chimpanzee.
Two crocodiles.
Three kings and a star make
Four . . . my new shoe size, just
Five days old. (I'm twice that now.) It's June—
Six more months until snow for sure.
Seven was lucky, not like
Eight, when I got glasses, better than
Nine, which felt Egyptian.

I'm ten now, which ends in
Zero. I've got
Four grandparents,
Three siblings,
Two parents and
One head with
Nothing to look at,
No place else to go.

ELIZA, AGE 10, HARLEM

I'm not small like they say,
those withered onions on the stoop
clucking their sorrowful tongues.
I'm concentrated. I'm a sweet
package of love. Jesus

says so, and He's better than angels
'cause He knows how to die;
He suffers the children
to come unto Him.
I can climb these stairs—

easy, even in T-straps. Yes,
I am my grandma's sugar pea
and someday I'm gonna pop

right out—and then, boys,
you better jump back!

LULLABY

(after Lorca's "Canción Tonta")

>> Mother, I want to rest in your lap again
>> as I did as a child.

Put your head here. How it floats,
heavy as your whole body was once.

>> If I fall asleep, I will be stiff
>> when I awake.

No stiffer than I.

>> But I want to lie down and do nothing
>> forever.

When I was angry with your father, I would take to my bed
like those fainting Victorian ladies.

>> I'm not angry at anyone.
>> Mostly I'm bored.

Boredom is useful for embroidery,
and a day of rest never hurt anyone.

>> Mother, I want the birthday supper of my childhood,
>> dripping with sauce.

Then you must lie down while I fix it!
Here, a pillow for your back.

>> I can't. The school bus is coming.
>> She'll be waiting at the corner.

Already? So soon!

DRIVING THROUGH

I know this scene: There's an engine
idling, without keys, just outside Mr. Nehi's
algebra class. I escape without notice,
past the frosted glass of the wood shop
and the ironclad lockers with their inscrutable hasps
that never shut clean. I know
the sweet hum of tires over asphalt,
green tunnels trickling sun,
proud elmfire before Dutch blight
vacuumed the corridors bare. And the rowdy kids
cluttering the curb, nappy heads bobbing,
squirrel blood streaking their sharpened sticks—
I know them, too. After all, this is the past
I'm driving through, and I know I'll end up
where I started, stiff-necked and dull-hearted,
cursing last night's red wine. So when

this girl, this woman-of-a-child
with her cheap hoops and barnyard breasts
snatches the door and flops onto the vinyl shouting
Let's ride!, I nod and head straight for
the police, although I can't quite recall
where the station is, law enforcement
not being part of my past.
Run me home first, she barks,
smiling, enjoying the bluff:
I need my good earrings.
I tell her we're almost there, which
we aren't, not by half, and how would I know
where she lives, anyway? We're both smiling
now; but only when we're good and lost,
traffic thinned to no more than

a mirage of flayed brick and scorched cement,
does she blurt out: *You're lying.*
True, I think; but lying is what I do best.
I turn toward her, meaning to confess
my wild affliction, my art. Instead

I hiss gibberish; she panics,
slams the door handle down and hurls

her ripe body into the street where
no one will ever remember seeing her
again.
                    What was that?
My husband bolts up from his pillow.
Just a dream, I stammer, head pounding
as I try to fall asleep again—
even though I knew that girl was lost
long before I went back to find her.

DESERT BACKYARD

Argentinean Pampas grass slices the careless ankle easily
and stings three days, most ardently at night.
Peruvian mulberry beguiles us
with purple pods called *pochettes d'amour:*
plump satchels that attack the heart.
The pear will not bear fruit; each spring
she stands arrayed in lace until
heat and wind bring that white affair

shamelessly down. We trim Egyptian sea grass
along the stone embrasure, prop up
flatulent elephant ears with sticks.
(Starved into vagrancy, the roses weep
gnawed petals.) The oleander, of course,
refuses to die. Burned in alleyways,
its sharp smoke cloys and raises welts,
fevered pockets of love leeched from the air.
Nowhere a delicacy, a pittance:

O deliver us
from magnificence.

DESK DREAMS

Tempe, Arizona

Honeyed wood with one eye widening the grain
just above my migratory pen.
I love this unconscious solitude—

the way whole afternoons belong to the cicada
calling down to her cousins
in yellow Mexico.

Paris, France

Janis on the radio, nonstop blues.
Midnight traffic from Gare du Nord,
surge and ebb of taxis and vegetable trucks
wafting through three stories of rain.
Places to get to. On the black desk
a full palette of notebooks
offering up their moonlit pages.

Research Triangle Park, North Carolina

White-bricked cell. One leafy, appreciative plant.
General issue desk and a balcony
leading nowhere, though the eye travels
deep into androgynous green.

Blue-ruled paper from grade school days.
I languish for hours
on the near side of a hyphen: great expectations
cut by the call
of a single prehensile jay.

Bellagio, Italy

Not a studio so much as an earthbound turret
or a periscope thrust
through the earth's omphalos:

Yoo-hoo, anybody there?
The walls are sleek as a shell's.

I will write my way out on a spiral of poems.
A mile down waits the lake,
chill Cyclopean blue;

while outside the door glimmers
the lesser mirror

of an artificial pond.
Is it true goldfish grow
to fit their containers?

Circles within circles:
Rapunzel, let down your hair.

Charlottesville, Virginia

Under crashed rafters
you stand,
honey in the ashes.

Your soaked plywood
and crazed veneer
aren't even worth

the hourly wage
of these men
in blue shirts

building boxes,
Salvage Experts trained
in the packing and storage

of household effects
singed by adversity,
anointed by the fireman's hose.

I save you by begging
sentimentality:
a female prerogative

I am grateful this once
to claim, since
tears will not serve

on a day as blue
as this one, the heavens
scrubbed and shining.

NOW

The glass shone cold
with water fresh

from somebody's old
"family spring" west

of the Blue Ridge.
I drank half

in one continuous
gulp—not

greed, but because
the day was hot.

Then, out of breath or
the telephone

rang, I don't remember—
I stopped. I put the glass down

to mist on the counter
as I warmed to whatever

errand required my
sensibilities.

I was gone
all day

and when I returned, there
it stood—forgotten, slippery

in a darkening
ring

of neglect—mute evidence
of my earlier thirst

now room temperature,
one half of pure

nothing. No small
task, then

to reach for the glass and
drink it all.

AGAINST FLIGHT

Everyone wants to go up—but no one can imagine
what it's like when the earth smoothes out, begins

to curve into its own implacable symbol.
Once you've adjusted to chilled footsoles,

what to do with your hands? Can so much wind
be comfortable? No sense

looking around when you can see
everywhere: There'll be no more clouds

worth reshaping into daydreams, no more
daybreaks to make you feel larger than life;

no eagle envy or fidgeting for a better view
from the eighteenth row in the theater . . .

no more theater, for that matter, and no
concerts, no opera or ballet. There'll be

no distractions except birds,
who never look you straight in the face,

and at the lower altitudes,
monarch butterflies—brilliant genetic engines

churning toward resurrection in a foreign land.
Who needs it? Each evening finds you

whipped to fringes, obliged to lie down
in a world of strangers, beyond perdition or pity—

bare to the stars, buoyant in the sweet sink of earth.

LOOKING UP FROM THE PAGE, I AM REMINDED OF THIS MORTAL COIL

Mercurial ribbon licking the cut lip of the Blue Ridge—
    daybreak
        or end, I can't tell
as long as I ignore the body's marching orders, as long as
        I am alive in air . . .

What good is the brain without traveling shoes?
We put our thoughts out there on the cosmos express
    and they hurtle on, tired and frightened,

bundled up in their worrisome
              shawls and gloves—I'm just

guessing here, but I suspect we don't
              travel easily at all, though we keep
              making better wheels—
                     smaller phones and wider webs,
                     ye olde significant glance
                            across the half-empty goblet
                            of Chardonnay. . . .

The blaze freshens,
              five or six miniature birds
              strike up the band.
Daybreak, of course; no more strobe and pink gels
              from the heavenly paint shop: just
house lights, play's over, time to gather your things and go home.

NOTES

Museum (1983)

Tou Wan Speaks to Her Husband, Liu Sheng: Liu Sheng, Prince Ching of Chung Shan, died in 113 B.C. He and his wife lived in the middle of the Western Han Dynasty. Their tombs were unearthed west of Mancheng, Hopei Province, in 1968.

Catherine of Alexandria: (died 307?). She rebuked the Roman emperor Galerius Valerius Maximinus, who then condemned her to be broken on the wheel. The wheel miraculously disintegrated.

Catherine of Siena: (1347–1380). A wool merchant's daughter, Catherine refused to marry. She received the stigmata and worked to secure peace between the Papacy and a divided Italy, dictating letters of advice to people all over Europe.

Shakespeare Say: Champion Jack Dupree, black American blues singer, toured extensively in Europe.

Banneker: Benjamin Banneker (1731–1806), first black man to devise an almanac and predict a solar eclipse accurately, was also appointed to the commission that surveyed and laid out what is now Washington, D.C.

Agosta the Winged Man and Rasha the Black Dove: Christian Schad (1894–1982) painted the two sideshow entertainers in Berlin in 1929.

Parsley: On October 2, 1937, Rafael Trujillo (1891–1961), dictator of the Dominican Republic, ordered 20,000 blacks killed because they could not pronounce the letter "r" in *perejil*, the Spanish word for parsley.

Grace Notes (1989)

The quotes introducing the five sections of this book are drawn from the following works: Toni Morrison, "The Site of Memory" (I.); David McFadden, *A Trip Around Lake Huron*, & Hélène Cixous, *Illa* (II.); Rita Dove, *The Other Side of the House* (III.); Claude McKay, "My House" (IV.); Cavafy, "The City" (V.).

Mother Love (1995)

The opening line to section II of "Persephone in Hell" owes its inspiration to a comment made by Hélène Cixous in a 1982 interview with Verena Andermatt Conley.

The epigraph to section V is taken from Adrienne Rich's adaptation from the Yiddish of Kadia Molodowsky.

On the Bus with Rosa Parks (1999)

"The Camel Comes to Us from the Barbarians": This allegorical poem was inspired by an Aesop fable entitled "The First Appearance of the Camel"; it relates how man's terror of this strange and powerful creature gradually turns to contempt once the means to control and domesticate the animal were discovered.

"There Came a Soul": Ivan Albright (1897–1983) began his painting of Ida Rogers in 1929. Although the model was a twenty-year-old wife and mother, the Chicago artist decided to portray her as a lonely old woman. Art scholars cite Albright's experience as a medical illustrator during World War I as a possible motive for his later preoccupation with old age.

"On the Bus with Rosa Parks": In 1995, during a convention in Williamsburg, Virginia, as the conferees were boarding buses to be driven to another site, my daughter leaned over and whispered, "Hey, we're on the bus with Rosa Parks!" Although the precipitating incident did not make it into a poem, the phrase haunted me—and so this meditation on history and the individual, image and essence was born. (By the way, Mrs. Parks took a seat in the front of the bus.)

"Claudette Colvin Goes to Work": Before Rosa Parks's historic refusal to move to the back of the bus in Montgomery, Alabama, on December 1, 1955, several other women had been arrested for violating that city's public transportation segregation laws. On March 2 of the same year, fifteen-year-old Claudette Colvin refused to yield her seat to white high school students. And on October 21, Mary Louise Smith was on her way home from a bad day when she was roused from daydreaming by an irate white passenger; she, too, did not vacate her seat voluntarily.

American Smooth (2004)

Frontispiece: The definitions of "American" and "smooth" are excerpted from *The American Heritage Dictionary of the English Language*, 3rd and 4th editions (Houghton Mifflin). The definition of "American Smooth" is my own.

All section epigraphs are remarks made by Lieutenant Commander Tuvok of the Federation Starship *Voyager*—a character in the television series *Star Trek: Voyager* (1995–2001).

"Quick," "Brown," "Fox": *The quick brown fox jumped over the lazy dog*. This sentence, which contains all the letters in the English alphabet and has been the delight of countless school children and the despair of many typists-in-training, was my inspiration for a multimedia piece that was auctioned at a gala benefiting the Virginia Center for the Creative Arts (VCCA) during the Foxfield Races in Charlottesville, Virginia, in 2002: a painted plywood fox, the words "Quick Brown Fox" parading along his arched spine, carried the three poems you see here: one rolled into his collar, one tucked into a saddlebag, one in a pouch tied to his tail.

"Soprano" is dedicated to the memory of Edmund Najera.

"Meditation at Fifty Yards, Moving Target" is dedicated to Gabriel Robins.

NOT WELCOME HERE: African-Americans clamoring to enlist for combat during World War I came up against the bulwark of Race: The American armed forces, segregated and intransigent, showed no trust in the combat-worthiness of the would-be soldiers, who languished stateside until the French, who knew no such squeamishness, asked for them. The celebrated 369th was the first regiment to arrive; by war's end, it had logged the longest time in continuous combat (191 days) and received a staggering number of medals (170 individual Croix de Guerre). It was also the first regiment to fight its way to the Rhine in 1918.

Grateful acknowledgment is made to two sources in particular: *Scott's Official History of the American Negro in the World War* (© 1919 by Emmett J. Scott) and *The Unknown Soldiers: Black American Troops in World War I* by Arthur E. Barbeau and Florette Henri (Temple University Press: © 1974 by Temple University).

"The Passage": Based on the diary and reminiscences of Orval Peyton, who welcomed me into his Tucson, Arizona, home one sunny afternoon in 1987.

"The Castle Walk": In 1913 James Europe and his Society Orchestra were engaged by the celebrated dance team Vernon and Irene Castle, whose brand of ballroom dancing was the rage among New York City's wealthy elite. The Castles ran a dance studio, Castle House, as well as the supper club San Souci.

"Ripont": The epigraph is from *The Unknown Soldiers: Black American Troops in World War I* by Arthur E. Barbeau and Florette Henri.

TWELVE CHAIRS: Most of these pieces—some in slightly different form—can be found carved on the backs of twelve marble chairs in the lobby of the Federal Court House in Sacramento, California as part of an installation by designer Larry Kirkland.

"Hattie McDaniel Arrives at the Coconut Grove": Hattie McDaniel was the first African-American to win an Oscar (Best Actress in a Supporting Role) for her portrayal of Mammy in the 1939 epic *Gone with the Wind*. For more on her life beyond that fateful evening, see Carlton Jackson's *Hattie: The Life of Hattie McDaniel* (Madison Books, Lanham, Md., 1990).

"From Your Valentine": Imprisoned by the Roman emperor Claudius for acting as an intermediary between forbidden lovers, the future saint Valentinus befriended the jailer's daughter and eventually cured her of her blindness. On the eve of his execution he left her a farewell note, signed "From your Valentine."

"Rhumba": The epigraph is taken from the opening lines of the song "Yo vengo aquí," written by Francisco Repilado (Compay Segundo) in 1922.

ACKNOWLEDGMENTS

"In the Old Neighborhood" was commissioned as the Phi Beta Kappa poem at Harvard University's 1993 commencement exercises and was published that same year in the introduction to Rita Dove's *Selected Poems*, Pantheon Press.

The Yellow House on the Corner (1980)

Some of these poems have appeared in the following magazines and anthologies:

Antaeus, The American Poetry Anthology, Eating the Menu, The Georgia Review, Intro 6, Miami Alumni, Missouri Review, New Honolulu Review, North American Review, Ohio Review, Paris Review, Pearl, Prairie Schooner, Snapdragon, Three Rivers Poetry Journal, and *The Virginia Quarterly Review.*

"Nigger Song: An Odyssey," "Adolescence—II," and "Planning the Perfect Evening" appeared originally in *Antaeus*. "Robert Schumann, or: Musical Genius Begins with Affliction" and "Small Town" appeared originally in *The Georgia Review*. "Adolescence—III" is reprinted from *Prairie Schooner*, Vol. 49, No. 1, by permission of University of Nebraska Press. Copyright © 1975 by University of Nebraska Press. "The Boast" by Rita Dove from *Intro 6*, edited by George Garrett. Copyright © 1974 by Associated Writing Programs. Reprinted by permission of Doubleday & Company, Inc.

"Adolescence II," "Adolescence III," "Upon Meeting Don L. Lee, In a Dream," "The Abduction," "The House Slave," "Corduroy Road," "Snow King," "1963," "Beauty and the Beast," and "The Bird Frau" first appeared in the letterpress chapbook *Ten Poems*, The Penumbra Press, Lisbon, Iowa, © 1977 by Rita Dove.

Museum (1983)

Some of these poems have appeared in the following magazines:

The Georgia Review: "The Hill Has Something to Say," "Receiving the Stigmata"; *Kenyon Review*: "Grape Sherbet"; *Massachusetts Review*: "Anti-Father," "Three Days of Forest, a River, Free"; *The Nation*: "The Ants of Argos"; *National Forum*: "The Fish in the Stone"; *New Orleans Review*: "The Left-Handed Cellist"; *Ontario Review*: "Eastern European Eclogues," "Parsley"; *Poetry*: "Agosta the Winged Man and Rasha the Black Dove," "Dusting," "November for Beginners" (© 1981 Modern Poetry Association), "Flirtation" (© 1982 Modern Poetry Association); *Poetry NOW*: "Lines Muttered in Sleep," "Tou Wan Speaks to Her Husband, Liu Sheng"; *The Reaper*: "At the German Writers Conference in Munich," "Primer for the Nuclear Age," "Shakespeare Say"; *Tesseract*: "Catherine of Alexandria," "Catherine of Siena," "Reading Hölderlin on the Patio with the Aid of a Dictionary."

The quote at the beginning of section II ("In the Bulrush") is from the song "Sun is shining" by Bob Marley. © 1977 Bob Marley Music Ltd. Used by permission.

Thomas and Beulah (1986)

These poems have appeared, sometimes in different versions, in the following magazines:

Agni Review: "Daystar," "Weathering Out"; *Callaloo*: "Company," "The House on Bishop Street," "Motherhood," "Nightmare," "One Volume Missing," "Promises," "Recovery," "Roast Possum," "Straw Hat," "Under the Viaduct, 1932"; *Cutbank*: "Aircraft," "Obedience", *The Georgia Review*: "Gospel"; *New England Review & Bread Loaf Quarterly*: "Courtship, Diligence," "The Oriental Ballerina"; *Nimrod*: "Magic," "Sunday Greens"; *Paris Review*: "Lightnin' Blues," "The Satisfaction Coal Company," "Wingfoot Lake"; *Ploughshares*: "Taking in Wash"; *Poetry*: "Pomade"; *The Reaper*: "A Hill of Beans," "Nothing Down," "Thomas at the Wheel."

The following poems appeared as a chapbook feature under the title *Mandolin* in *Ohio Review 28*: "The Event," "Variation on Pain," "Jiving," "The Zeppelin Factory," "Courtship," "Refrain," "Variation on Guilt," "Compendium," "Definition in the Face of Unnamed Fury," "Aurora Borealis," "The Charm," and "The Stroke."

"The Great Palaces of Versailles," "Pomade," and "The Oriental Ballerina" appeared in *New American Poets of the Eighties* (Wampeter Press, 1984). "Dusting" first appeared in *Poetry* and subsequently in *Pushcart Prize: VII* (Pushcart Press, 1982), *Museum* (Carnegie-Mellon University Press, 1983), and *The Morrow Anthology of Younger American Poets* (1985).

"A Hill of Beans" and "Wingfoot Lake" also appeared in *The Bread Loaf Anthology of Contemporary American Poetry* (University Press of New England, 1985).

Grace Notes (1989)

These poems first appeared, sometimes in different versions, in the following publications:

Black Scholar: "Poem in Which I Refuse Contemplation"; *The Boston Review*: "Flash Cards," "Saints"; *Caprice*: "Medusa"; *Chelsea*: "Dialectical Romance," "Particulars"; *Clockwatch Review*: "Mississippi," "Stitches"; *Cottonwood*: "Summit Beach, 1921"; *Erato*: "On the Road to Damascus"; *Five A.M.*: "After Reading *Mickey in the Night Kitchen* for the Third Time Before Bed"; *The Georgia Review*: "Horse and Tree"; *Graham House Review*: "In the Museum," "Pastoral"; *Hayden's Ferry Review*: "After Storm"; *High Plains Literary Review*: "Backyard, 6 a.m.," "Ozone"; *The Iowa Review*: "Turning Thirty, I Contemplate Students Bicycling Home"; *The Michigan Quarterly Review*: "Arrow"; *Partisan Review*: "Crab-Boil"; *Ploughshares*: "Fantasy and Science Fiction," "Hully Gully," "Obbligato"; *Poetry*: "Ars Poetica," "The Breathing, The Endless News," "Old Folk's Home, Jerusalem," "The Wake";

Poetry Now: "Quaker Oats," "Silos"; *Prairie Schooner*: "The Buckeye," "The Other Side of the House"; *River Styx*: "Uncle Millet"; *South Coast Poetry Journal*: "Sisters"; *The Seneca Review*: "Your Death"; *The Southern Review*: "Dog Days, Jerusalem," "Fifth Grade Autobiography," "The Gorge"; *Southwest Review*: "À l'Opéra," "Lint," "The Royal Workshops"; *Telescope*: "Watching *Last Year at Marienbad* at Roger Haggerty's House in Auburn, Alabama"; *TriQuarterly*: "And Counting," "Canary," "Genie's Prayer under the Kitchen Sink," "In a Neutral City," "The Island Women of Paris"; *The Yale Review*: "Dedication."

"Canary" and "After Reading *Mickey in the Night Kitchen* for the Third Time Before Bed" were also published in *Early Ripening: American Women's Poetry Now*, edited by Marge Piercy, Pandora Press (New York & London, 1987).

"Backyard, 6 a.m.," "The Breathing, The Endless News," "Genetic Expedition," "Horse and Tree," "The Other Side of the House," "Pastoral," and "After Reading *Mickey in the Night Kitchen* for the Third Time Before Bed" appeared with seven collotype-printed photographs by Tamarra Kaida in a fine press edition entitled *The Other Side of the House*, published by Pyracantha Press (Arizona State University, Tempe, Arizona) in 1988.

"Ozone" was also printed as a broadside with a lithograph by Ron Gasowski in *The Dance of Death*, a portfolio produced by John Risseeuw at Pyracantha Press in 1989.

Mother Love (1995)

These poems first appeared, sometimes in different versions, in the following periodicals:

American Poetry Review: "Afield," "Demeter, Waiting," *"Wiederkehr"*; *Atlantic Monthly*: "Used"; *Black Warrior Review*: "Primer," "Party Dress for a First Born," "The Narcissus Flower," "Grief: The Council," "Mother Love," "Breakfast of Champions," "Lamentations," "Nature's Itinerary," "Lost Brilliance"; *Caprice*: "History"; *Callaloo*: "Heroes"; *The Georgia Review*: "Statistic: The Witness"; *The Gettysburg Review*: "Persephone in Hell"; *High Plains Literary Review*: "The Search" (as "Blown apart . . ."); *Mississippi Review*: "Exit," "Golden Oldie," "Wiring Home"; *Ms.* magazine: "Persephone Abducted"; *Parnassus*: "The Bistro Styx"; *Ploughshares*: "Missing," "Rusks," "Teotihuacán," "Blue Days" (as "Under Pressure . . ."); *Poetry*: "Demeter Mourning" (as "Sonnet"), "Demeter's Prayer to Hades," "Protection," "Her Island"; *Sequoia*: "Persephone, Falling," "Hades' Pitch" (as "Persephone Underground"); *Sojourner*: "Sonnet in Primary Colors"; *TriQuarterly*: "Political."

An earlier version of the foreword, "An Intact World," was published in *A Formal Feeling Comes—Poems in Form by Contemporary Women*, edited by Annie Finch, Story Line Press, 1994. This anthology also contains the poems "Hades' Pitch" (as "Persephone Underground"), "History," "Political," and "The Search" (as "Blown Apart by Loss . . .")

On the Bus with Rosa Parks (1999)

These poems first appeared in the following publications:

Agni Review: "Cameos"; *American Poetry Review:* "Best Western Motor Lodge, AAA Approved"; *The American Scholar:* "Maple Valley Branch Library, 1967"; *Callaloo:* "Dawn Revisited"; *Chelsea:* "The Musician Talks about 'Process'"; *Doubletake:* "Parlor"; *The Georgia Review:* "On Veronica"; *The Gettysburg Review:* "Ghost Walk" and "The Camel Comes to Us from the Barbarians"; *International Quarterly:* "I Cut My Finger Once on Purpose"; *Meridian:* "The Peach Orchard"; *The New Yorker:* "Incarnation in Phoenix"; *Parnassus:* "Against Repose" and "Götterdämmerung"; *Poetry:* "For Sophie, Who'll Be in First Grade in the Year 2000," "Testimonial," and "The Venus of Willendorf"; *Poetry Review* (U.K.): "Singsong"; *The Progressive:* "Black on a Saturday Night"; *Slate:* "Against Self-Pity," "Revenant," and "Sunday"; *USA Weekend:* "Freedom, Bird's-Eye View" and "My Mother Enters the Work Force."

The title sequence, "On the Bus with Rosa Parks," was first published as a special section in *The Georgia Review*, Winter 1998.

"Lady Freedom Among Us" was read by the author at the ceremony commemorating the 200th anniversary of the United States Capitol and the restoration of the Statue of Freedom to the Capitol dome on October 23, 1993, and first published in the *Congressional Record* of the same day. It was subsequently commissioned as the four millionth volume of the University of Virginia Libraries in a fine press edition by Janus Press, West Burke, Vermont, 1994, and at the same time made globally accessible by the University of Virginia in a multimedia version on the Internet. "Lady Freedom Among Us" also appeared in *The Poet's World*, a volume of the author's poet laureate lectures at the Library of Congress (Library of Congress, 1995), and in several other publications.

"The First Book" appeared first in *The Language of Life*, edited by Bill Moyers, 1995. It also was available as an American Library Association poster and bookmark.

"There Came a Soul" appeared first in *Transforming Vision: Writers on Art*, edited by Edward Hirsch. The Art Institute of Chicago, 1994.

"Black on a Saturday Night" and "Singsong" (as "Song") are also part of *Seven for Luck*, a song cycle for soprano and orchestra, lyrics by Rita Dove, music by John Williams, and appeared in the program for the song cycle's world premiere with the Boston Symphony Orchestra at Tanglewood, July 25, 1998.

The epigraph to the title sequence is from Simon Schama's essay "Clio at the Multiplex," *The New Yorker*, January 19, 1998.

American Smooth (2004)

These poems first appeared—some in slightly different form—in the following publications:

American Poetry Review: "The Castle Walk," "Noble Sissle's Horn," "Ripont," "The Return of Lieutenant James Reese Europe," and "Variation on Reclamation"; *The American Scholar:* "Looking Up from the Page, I am Reminded of This Mortal Coil"; *Callaloo:* "Desk Dreams" and "Fox Trot Fridays"; *Columbia Magazine:* "Lullaby"; *The Georgia Review:* "Against Flight," "Describe Yourself in Three Words or Less," "Rhumba," and "Samba Summer"; *The Gettysburg Review:* "Quick," "Brown," and "Fox"; *International Quarterly:* "Desert Backyard" and "Eliza, Age 10, Harlem"; *Meridian:* "Count to Ten and We'll Be There"; *Mid-American Review:* "Driving Through"; *The New Yorker:* "All Souls'," "American Smooth," and "Hattie McDaniel Arrives at the Coconut Grove"; *Ploughshares:* "Bolero," "Mercy," and "Now"; *Poetry:* "Cozy Apologia," "Evening Primrose," "I Have Been a Stranger in a Strange Land," "Reverie in Open Air," "The Seven Veils of Salomé," and "Soprano"; *The Progressive:* "From Your Valentine"; *River Styx:* "Alfonzo Prepares to Go Over the Top"; *Shenandoah:* "Heart to Heart" and "Meditation at Fifty Yards, Moving Target"; *Slate:* "Blues in Half-Tones, 3/4 Time," "Ta Ta Cha Cha," and "Two for the Montrose Drive-In"; *The Southern Review:* "La Chapelle. 92nd Division. Ted."

"Chocolate," "Eliza, Age 10, Harlem," "Evening Primrose," and "Soprano" appeared in the chapbook *Evening Primrose: Selected Poems*, Tunheim Santrizos Company (Minneapolis, Minn.), 1998.

"Chocolate" is also part of *Seven for Luck*, a song cycle for soprano and orchestra, lyrics by Rita Dove, music by John Williams, and first appeared in the program of the song cycle's world premiere with the Boston Symphony at Tanglewood, July 25, 1998.

"Sic Itur Ad Astra" appeared in the May 7, 1995, issue of *The Washington Post Sunday Magazine*, in conjunction with the cover article by Walt Harrington titled "The Shape of Her Dreaming: Rita Dove Writes a Poem."

IN GRATITUDE

Heartfelt thanks to Bonnie O'Connell for publishing my first chapbook in 1977; to Gerald Costanzo at Carnegie Mellon University Press for shepherding the three collections that followed; to Robin Desser at Pantheon Books, who later assembled those three books into one volume; and to Jill Bialosky, who brought this current compilation to fruition. Also in remembrance of George Garrett, the first editor who afforded me a national audience when, in 1974, he chose a poem of mine for *Intro 6;* and in grateful memory of Carol Houck Smith, my generous and patient editor whose vision and advice accompanied the four books published by W. W. Norton between 1989 and 2004.

I wouldn't be where and who I am today without my husband Fred Viebahn, always my first and foremost reader.

INDEX OF TITLES AND FIRST LINES

Abduction, The, 33
a boy, at most, 202
A cornet's soul is in its bell—, 371
Adolescence—I, 43
Adolescence—II, 43
Adolescence—III, 44
Afield, 259
A flower in a weedy field, 227
A friend, blonde pigtail flung over an ear, 214
After all, there's no need, 107
After Reading Mickey in the Night Kitchen *for the Third Time Before Bed*, 193
After Storm, 181
Against Flight, 416
Against Repose, 319
Against Self-Pity, 320
Agosta the Winged Man and Rasha the Black Dove, 84
Ain't got a reason, 37
Aircraft, 129
A letter from my mother was waiting, 176
Alfonzo Prepares to Go Over the Top, 370
All Souls', 345
All the toothy Fräuleins are left behind, 56
À l'Opéra, 214
Already the desert sky had packed, 181
Although it is night, I sit in the bathroom, waiting, 43
American Smooth, 358
And Counting, 203
And it was almost a boy who undid, 46
Anniversary, 148
Anti-Father, 96
Ants of Argos, The, 64
are walking towards me, 23
Are you having a good time?, 233
Argentinean Pampas grass slices the careless ankle easily, 412
Aristocrat among patriarchs, this, 67
Around us: blazed stones, closed ground, 271
Arrow, 200
Ars Poetica, 199
As if, after High Street, 330
"A soldier waits until he's called—then, 372
A straw reed climbs the car antenna, 321
As usual, legend got it all, 65
At the dinner table, before the baked eggplant, 44
At the edge of the mariner's, 109
At the German Writers Conference in Munich, 86
At the outset, hysteria, 36
At two, the barnyard settled, 35
Aurora Borealis, 130
A yellow scarf runs through his fingers, 142

Back when the earth was new, 298
Backyard, 6 a.m., 195
Banneker, 81
Beauty and the Beast, 53
Bed, where are you flying to?, 408
Belinda's Petition, 31
Beneath the brushed wing of the mallard, 215
Best Western Motor Lodge, AAA Approved, 315
Billie Holiday's burned voice, 213
Bird Frau, The, 13
Bistro Styx, The, 252
Black chest hairs, soft sudden mass, 109
Black on a Saturday Night, 303
Blown apart by loss, she let herself go—, 232
Blue Days, 257
Blues in Half-Tones, 3/4 Time, 395
Boast, The, 44
Boccaccio: The Plague Years, 71
Bolero, 391
Breakfast of Champions, 237
Breathing, The Endless News, The, 193
Broke-leg cakewalk of the drunken uncles, 394
Brown, 349
Buckeye, The, 170
but isn't talking, 66

Camel Comes to Us from the Barbarians, The, 307
Cameos, 281
Canary, 213
Can't use no teenager, especially, 333
Castle Walk, The, 363
Catherine of Alexandria, 69
Catherine of Siena, 70
Centipede, 94
Champagne, 24
Charm, The, 132
Chocolate, 391
Cholera, 36
Chronology, 160
Claudette Colvin Goes to Work, 331
Climb, 64
Climbing In, 331
Come here, I want to show you something, 16
Company, 157
Compendium, 128
Contrary to, 96
Copper Beech, The, 67
Corduroy Road, 57
Count it anyway he wants—, 122
Count to Ten and We'll Be There, 409
Courtship, 120
Courtship, Diligence, 142
Cozy Apologia, 352

Crab-Boil, 172
Cut a cane that once, 82

Darling, the plates have been cleared away, 53
David Walker (1785–1830), 32
Dawn Revisited, 299
Daystar, 149
Dedication, 199
Definition in the Face of Unnamed Fury, 128
Delft, 83
Demeter Mourning, 258
Demeter's Prayer to Hades, 267
Demeter, Waiting, 263
Deprived of learning and, 69
Describe Yourself in Three Words or Less, 396
Desert Backyard, 412
Desk Dreams, 413
Dialectical Romance, 204
does not show his, 54
Dog Days, Jerusalem, 183
don't lower your eyes, 324
Driving Through, 411
Dusting, 144

Each evening I see my breasts, 194
Each hurt swallowed, 143
Early fall in the fields a slow day's drive south, 377
Early Morning on the Tel Aviv–Haifa Freeway, 105
Eastern European Eclogues, 106
Eliza, Age 10, Harlem, 409
Enactment, The, 333
Even at night the air rang and rang, 71
Evening Primrose, 407
Evening, the bees fled, the honeysuckle, 218
Event, The, 117
Ever since they'd left the Tennessee ridge, 117
Everybody who's anybody longs to be a tree—, 192
Every day a wilderness—no, 144
Every god is lonely, an exile, 193
Everyone wants to go up—but no one can imagine, 416
Everything civilized will whistle before, 183
Everything's a metaphor, some wise, 265
Exactly at six every evening I go, 183
Exeunt the Viols, 108
Exit, 259
Exposed to light, 316

Fantasy and Science Fiction, 174
Father out Walking on the Lawn, A, 97
Fiammetta Breaks Her Peace, 72
Fifth Grade Autobiography, 169
Finally, overcast skies. I've crossed a hemisphere, 237
Fine evening may I have, 120
First Book, The, 295
First Kiss, 46
Fish in the Stone, The, 63
Five Elephants, 23
Five rings light your approach across, 97

Flash Cards, 172
Flat, with variations. Not, 83
Flirtation, 107
For a fifteen-year-old there was plenty, 296
For Kazuko, 53
For Sophie, Who'll Be in First Grade in the Year 2000, 325
Fox, 350
Fox Trot Fridays, 347
Freedom: Bird's-Eye View, 297
Freedom Ride, 330
Free to travel, he still couldn't be shown how lucky, 32
From nothing comes nothing, 395
From Your Valentine, 399

Genetic Expedition, 194
Genie's Prayer under the Kitchen Sink, 209
Geometry, 23
Ghost Walk, 322
Golden Oldie, 238
Gorge, The, 211
Gospel, 133
Götterdämmerung, 321
Got up, 364
Grape Sherbet, 91
Great Palaces of Versailles, The, 150
Great Uncle Beefheart, 55
Green sludge of a riverbank, 131
Grew hair for fun, 84
Grief: The Council, 235

Hades' Pitch, 251
Hair and bacon grease, pearl button, 209
Happenstance, 15
Hattie McDaniel Arrives at the Coconut Grove, 392
Headdress, 153
Heading North, straw hat, 118
Headless girl so ill at ease on the bed, 231
Heart to Heart, 351
He asked if she believed in God, 204
He avoided the empty millyards, 126
He comes toward me with lashless eyes, 18
He drums the piano wood, 78
He'd slip a rubber band around a glass of rye, 175
He gave up fine cordials and, 128
He lets her pick the color, 123
He liked to joke and all of his jokes were practical, 93
He only wanted me for happiness, 251
Her Island, 271
Heroes, 227
He's tucked his feet into corduroy scuffs, 155
Hill Has Something to Say, The, 66
Hill of Beans, A, 145
His Shirt, 54
History, 265
Honeyed wood with one eye widening the grain, 413

Horse and Tree, 192
House on Bishop Street, The, 148
House Slave, The, 31
How she sat there, 334
Hully Gully, 173

I acknowledge my status as a stranger, 407
I am the daughter who went out with the girls, 266
I could pick anything and think of you—, 352
I Cut My Finger Once on Purpose, 293
I don't know if I helped him up, 34
If I could just touch your ankle, he whispers, there,
    251
if I whispered to the moon, 248
Ignore me. This request is knotted—, 199
"I have been a stranger in a strange land," 346
Ike, 84
I know this scene: There's an engine, 411
I learned the spoons from, 304
I made it home early, only to get, 238
Imagine you wake up, 299
I miss that corridor drenched in shadow, 260
I'm no baby. There's no grizzly man, 293
I'm not small like they say, 409
I'm not the kind of person who praises, 396
In a far far land where men are men, 16
In a Neutral City, 205
Incarnation in Phoenix, 311
In math I was the whiz kid, keeper, 172
Intact World, An, 223
In the beginning was the dark, 181
In the Bulrush, 82
In the city, under the saw-toothed leaves of an oak,
    119
In the large hall of the Hofbräuhaus, 86
In the Lobby of the Warner Theatre, Washington,
    D.C., 335
In the Museum, 202
In the Old Neighborhood, 3
In the old neighborhood, each funeral parlor, 18
In the sixth grade I was chased home by, 231
In this stucco house there is nothing but air, 24
Intolerable: that civilized word, 329
Into this paradise of pain she strides, 311
In water-heavy nights behind grandmother's porch,
    43
I prove a theorem and the house expands, 23
I remember my foot in its frivolous slipper, 233
Irene says it's the altitude, 257
I say there is no memory of him, 318
I should have known if you gave me flowers, 47
I sit, and sit, and will my thoughts, 336
Island Women of Paris, The, 213
I stood at 6 a.m. on the wharf, 36
It began with A—years before in a room, 14
It gets you nowhere but deeper into, 320
It is Sunday, day of roughhousing, 38
I told her: enough is enough, 235
It's neither red, 351

It's time you learned something, 92
It was not as if he didn't try, 55
It wasn't bliss. What was bliss, 346
I walk out the kitchen door, 191
I was four in this photograph fishing, 169
I was ill, lying on my bed of old papers, 25
I was not quite twenty when I first went down, 241
I was standing in the doorway, 397
I will build you a house, 68
I will marry this clump of flowers, 45
I wrote stubbornly into the evening, 47
I've got to go, 205
I've watched them, mother, and I know, 72

Jiving, 118
Just when hope withers, a reprieve is granted, 259

Kadava Kumbis Devise a Way to Marry for Love,
    The, 45
Kentucky, 1833, 38

La Chapelle. 92nd Division. Ted., 373
Lady Freedom Among Us, 324
Lamentations, 264
late, in aqua and ermine, gardenias, 392
Later he'll say Death stepped right up, 135
Left-Handed Cellist, The, 109
Lest the wolves loose their whistles, 252
Lightnin' Blues, 127
Like an otter, but warm, 192
Like martial swans in spring paraded against the city
    sky's, 169
Lines Muttered in Sleep, 109
Lint, 215
Little Cuyahoga's done up left town, 211
Locked in bathrooms for hours, 173
Look, a baby one! Wink of fuzz, 348
Looking Up from the Page, I Am Reminded of This
    Mortal Coil, 417
Lord, Lord. No rest, 329
Lost Brilliance, 260
Lucille among the flamingos, 281
Lullaby, 410

Magic, 141
Maple Valley Branch Library, 1967, 296
Meditation at Fifty Yards, Moving Target, 356
Medusa, 205
Menial twilight sweeps the storefronts along Lex-
    ington, 331
Mercurial ribbon licking the cut lip of the Blue
    Ridge—, 417
Missing, 266
Mississippi, 181
Mister Minister, I found, 105
Motherhood, 147
Mother, I want to rest in your lap again, 410
Mother Love, 236
Music across the lake? Impossible . . . , 374

Musician Talks About "Process," The, 304
My daughter spreads her legs, 193
My Father's Telescope, 94
My Mother Enters the Work Force, 303

Narcissus Flower, The, 233
Nature's Itinerary, 257
Neither rosy nor prim, 407
Nestor's Bathtub, 65
Never point your weapon, keep your finger, 356
Nexus, 47
Nigger Song: An Odyssey, 19
Nightmare, 155
Night Watch, 24
Noble Sissle's Horn, 371
No bright toy, 325
No front yard to speak of, 148
No matter where I turn, she is there, 234
No one can help him anymore, 157
Notes from a Tunisian Journal, 51
Nothing can console me. You may bring silk, 258
Nothing comes to mind, 319
Nothing Down, 123
Nothing nastier than a white person!, 150
Not the ratcheting crescendo of Ravel's bright
    winds, 391
November for Beginners, 77
Now, 415
No. Who can bear it. Only someone, 263
Nudged by bees, morning brightens to detail, 195

Ö, 58
Obbligato, 214
Obedience, 150
Old Folk's Home, Jerusalem, 218
One by one, the words, 77
One chimpanzee, 409
One narcissus among the ordinary beautiful, 232
One spring the circus gave, 145
One, two—no, five doves, 347
One Volume Missing, 131
On her 36th birthday, Thomas had shown her, 156
On my knees in the dark I looked out, 174
On the day that will always belong to you, 186
On the radio a canary bewailed her luck, 127
On the Road to Damascus, 217
On Veronica, 316
Open it, 295
Oriental Ballerina, The, 158
Other Side of the House, The, 191
Out where crows dip to their kill, 259
Ozone, 183

Palomino, horse of shadows, 315
Pamela, 35
Panel of gray silk. Liquefied ashes. Dingy percale
    tugged over, 334
Papa called her Pearl when he came home, 141
Parlor, 294

Parsley, 110
Particulars, 185
Party Dress for a First Born, 231
Passage, The, 364
Pastoral, 192
Patrons talk and talk and nothing, 214
Peach Orchard, The, 318
Pearls, 47
Persephone Abducted, 234
Persephone, Falling, 232
Persephone in Hell, 241
Pithos, 64
Poem in Which I Refuse Contemplation, 176
Political, 263
Pomade, 152
Pond, Porch-View: Six p.m., Early Spring, The, 336
Practice makes perfect, the old folks said, 141
Primer, 231
Primer for the Nuclear Age, 109
Promises, 143
Proof casts a shadow, 383
Protection, 231

QE2. Transatlantic Crossing. Third Day, 334
Quaker Oats, 171
Quick, 348

Raccoons have invaded the crawl space, 3
Reading Hölderlin on the Patio with the Aid of a
    Dictionary, 77
Receiving the Stigmata, 70
Recovery, 155
Refrain, 121
Return of Lieutenant James Reese Europe, The, 374
Revenant, 315
Reverie in Open Air, 407
Rhumba, 400
Ripont, 377
Roast Possum, 134
Robert Schumann, Or: Musical, Genius Begins with
    Affliction, 14
Roofless houses, cartons of chalk, 51
Rosa, 334
Roses, 92
Royal Workshops, The, 216
Rusks, 266

Sahara Bus Trip, The, 51
Sailor in Africa, The, 101
Saints, 209
Samba Summer, 394
Satisfaction Coal Company, The, 136
Schad paced the length of his studio, 84
Search, The, 232
Secret Garden, The, 25
Seven Veils of Salomé, The, 397
Sexless, my brother flies, 95
Shakespeare Say, 78
Shape the lips to an o, say a, 58

She arrived as near to virginal, 317
She cried out for Mama, who did not, 234
She discovered she felt better, 185
She dreams the baby's so small she keeps, 147
She kneels on a workbench, 308
She knew what, 350
She liked mornings the best—Thomas gone, 146
She's dreaming, 155
She sweeps the kitchen floor of the river bed her
    husband saw fit, 152
She used to pull them, 209
She walked alone, as she did every morning, 46
She wanted a little room for thinking, 149
She wants to hear, 154
She was thinner, with a mannered gauntness, 252
Sic Itur Ad Astra, 408
Sightseeing, 16
Silos, 169
Singsong, 293
Sisters, 175
Sisters: Swansong, The, 403
Sit Back, Relax, 329
skim from curb to curb like regatta, 213
Slave's Critique of Practical Reason, The, 37
Small Town, 15
Snow King, The, 16
Snow would be the easy, 77
Someday we'll talk about the day lily, 205
Someone is sitting in the red house, 15
Someone's Blood, 36
Song. Summer, 95
Sonnet in Primary Colors, 258
Son, The, 56
Soprano, 353
Spy, 46
Starting up behind them, 345
Statistic: The Witness, 234
Stitches, 201
Stone kettles on the beach by Sidon, 216
Straw Hat, 119
Stroke, The, 135
Suite for Augustus, A, 25
Summit Beach, 1921, 165
Sunday, 305
Sunday Greens, 154
Sunday Night at Grandfather's, 93
Swing low so I, 133

Taking in Wash, 141
Ta Ta Cha Cha, 347
"Teach Us to Number Our Days," 18
Teeth, 331
Teotihuacán, 264
Testimonial, 298
Thank the stars there's a day, 347
That dragonfly, bloated, pinned, 128
That shy angle of his daughter's head—, 131
That smokestack, for instance, 150
That winter I stopped loving the President, 25

The bells, the cannons, the houses black with crepe,
    33
The bolero, silk-tassled, the fuchsia, 53
The conspiracy's to make us thin. Size threes, 265
The day? Memorial, 91
The days pass. Night floats, 399
The dogs have nothing better, 80
The eminent scholar "took the bull by the horns,"
    200
The first horn lifts its arm over the dew-lit grass, 31
The fish in the stone, 63
The glass shone cold, 415
The grain elevators have stood empty for years, 171
The green lamp flares on the table, 13
The hat on the table, 153
The Indian guide explains to the group of poets,
    264
Their father was a hunting man, 305
The man inside the mandolin, 121
The natives here have given up their backyards, 24
Then Came Flowers, 47
The Negro beach jumped to the twitch, 165
The neighbors who never, 322
The oldest joke, 94
The path to ABC Business School, 303
The possum's a greasy critter, 134
There are two white captains, 101
There Came a Soul, 317
There is a corridor of light, 182
There is a parrot imitating spring, 110
There is a way to enter a field, 70
There stood the citadel—nothing left, 64
There was a man spent seven years in hell's
    circles—, 263
The shore is cabbage green and reeks, 105
"The situation is intolerable," 329
The sun flies over the madrigals, 297
They called us, 132
They'd positioned her—two attendants flanking the
    wheelchair—, 335
They say I was struck down by the voice of an angel,
    217
The zeppelin factory, 125
Thirty miles to the only decent restaurant, 199
This alone is what I wish for you: knowledge, 267
This far south such crippling, 130
This is for the woman with one black wing, 258
This is how it happened, 266
This is no place for lilac, 303
This is the one we called, 175
This is the weather of change, 184
This Life, 13
This lonely beautiful word, 373
This melodious, 106
This nutmeg stick of a boy in loose trousers!, 51
This one is enormous: rough-cut, 307
This, then, the river he had to swim, 138
Thomas at the Wheel, 138
Three Days of Forest, a River, Free, 80

Throw open the shutters, 264
To Bed, 97
Too frail for combat, he stands, 129
To the honorable Senate and House, 31
Tou Wan Speaks to Her Husband, Liu Sheng, 68
Transport of Slaves from Maryland to Mississippi, The, 34
Turning Thirty, I Contemplate Students Bicycling Home, 184
Twelve years to the day, 148
twirls on the tips of a carnation, 158
Two for the Montrose Drive-In, 354
Two strings, one pierced cry, 118

Uncle Millet, 175
Under pressure Mick tells me one, 257
Under the Viaduct, 1932, 126
Upon Meeting Don L. Lee, In a Dream, 18
Used, 265

Variation on Gaining a Son, 131
Variation on Guilt, 122
Variation on Pain, 118
Variation on Reclamation, 374
Velvet fruit, exquisite square, 391
Venus of Willendorf, The, 308

Wake, The, 187
Watching Last Year at Marienbad *at Roger Haggerty's House in Auburn, Alabama*, 182
Weathering Out, 146
We died one by one, 403
We learned about the state tree, 170
Well of course I'm not worth it but neither is, 203
We passed through, 294
We six pile in, the engine churning ink, 19

We strike camp on that portion of road completed, 57
We trained in the streets: the streets where we came from, 376
We turn off, 97
We were dancing—it must have, 358
What did he do except lie, 81
What to do with a day, 136
When I was young, the moon spoke in riddles, 293
When skin opens, 201
When the boys came home, everything stopped, 13
When you appeared it was as if, 15
When you hit, 353
Where can I find Moon Avenue, 315
Who can forget the attitude of mothering?, 236
Why do I remember the sky, 172
Why I Turned Vegetarian, 105
Why you look good in every color!, 349
Wiederkehr, 251
Wingfoot Lake, 156
Wiring Home, 252
With Dad gone, Mom and I worked, 44
with their throb and yearn, their sad, 108
With the storm moved on the next town, 94

You came with a cello in one hand, 109
You can't accuse this group, 363
You have broken the path of the dragonfly, 47
Your absence distributed itself, 187
Your Death, 186
You walked the length of Italy, 70
yo vengo aquí   I come here, 400

Zeppelin Factory, The, 125